TEACHING TENNIS

Steps to Success

Jim Brown, PhD
McNeese University
Lake Charles, Louisiana

Leisure Press
Champaign, Illinois

Library of Congress Cataloging-in-Publication Data

Brown, Jim, 1940-
    Teaching tennis : steps to success / Jim Brown.
      p.   cm. — (Steps to success activity series)
    Bibliography: p.
    ISBN 0-88011-319-7
    1. Tennis—Study and teaching. I. Title. II. Series.
  GV991.5.B76 1989
796.342'07—dc19   88-9428
                                                     CIP

Developmental Editor: Judy Patterson Wright, PhD; **Production Director:** Ernie Noa; **Copy Editor:** Peter Nelson; **Assistant Editors:** Kathy Kane and Robert King; **Proofreader:** Laurie McGee; **Typesetter:** Yvonne Winsor; **Text Design:** Keith Blomberg; **Text Layout:** Tara Welsch; **Cover Design:** Jack Davis; **Cover Photo:** Bill Morrow; **Illustrations By:** Raneé Rogers and Gretchen Walters; **Printed By:** United Graphics, Inc.

Instructional Designer for the Steps to Success Activity Series: Joan N. Vickers, EdD, University of Calgary, Calgary, Alberta, Canada

ISBN: 0-88011-319-7

Copyright © 1989 by Leisure Press

All rights reserved. Except for use in a review, the reproduction or utilization of this work in any form or by any electronic, mechanical, or other means, now known or hereafter invented, including xerography, photocopying and recording, and in any information retrieval system, is forbidden without the written permission of the publisher.

Notice: Permission to reproduce the following material is granted to instructors and agencies who have purchased *Teaching Tennis: Steps to Success*: page 171 (Postmatch Scouting Form); page 172 (Error Chart); page 173 (Winning Shot Chart); page 181 (Skill Test Form); page 198 (Scope and Teaching Sequence); pages 202-203 (Individual Program); and page 207 (Lesson Plan). The reproduction of other parts of this book is expressly forbidden by the above copyright notice. Instructors or agencies who have not purchased *Teaching Tennis: Steps to Success* may not reproduce any material.

Printed in the United States of America   10 9 8 7 6 5 4

Leisure Press
A Division of Human Kinetics Publishers
Box 5076, Champaign, IL 61825-5076
1-800-747-4457

Canada: Human Kinetics Publishers, Box 24040, Windsor, ON N8Y 4Y9
1-800-465-7301 (in Canada only)

Europe: Human Kinetics Publishers (Europe) Ltd., P.O. Box IW14, Leeds LS16 6TR, England
0532-781708

Australia: Human Kinetics Publishers, P.O. Box 80, Kingswood 5062, South Australia
618-374-0433

New Zealand: Human Kinetics Publishers, P.O. Box 105-231, Auckland 1
(09) 309-2259

Contents

Series Preface		v
Preface		vii
Implementing the Steps to Success Staircase		ix
Class Management and Organization		1
Step 1	Handling the Racket	9
Step 2	Preparing to Hit	16
Step 3	Groundstrokes: Forehand and Backhand	27
Step 4	Groundstroke Combinations	46
Step 5	Beginner's (Punch) Serve	54
Step 6	Full-Swing Serve	67
Step 7	Three-Shot Singles	81
Step 8	Beginner's Volley	85
Step 9	Lob	96
Step 10	Smash	103
Step 11	Volley–Lob–Smash Combinations	113
Step 12	Advanced Volley	118
Step 13	Half-Volley	131
Step 14	Drop Shot	137
Step 15	Singles: Strategy and Formats for Competition	143
Step 16	Doubles and Mixed Doubles: Strategy and Drills	153
Step 17	Adjusting to Opponents and Conditions	161
Step 18	Concentration	164
Step 19	Learning by Watching	170
Gymnasium and Classroom Activities		175
Evaluation Ideas		179
Test Bank		183
Appendices		193
Appendix A	Knowledge Structure of Tennis (Overview)	194
Appendix B.1	Sample Scope and Teaching Sequence	196
Appendix B.2	Scope and Teaching Sequence (Blank)	197
Appendix C.1	Sample Individual Program	199
Appendix C.2	Individual Program (Blank)	202
Appendix C.3	Sample Group Program	204
Appendix D.1	Sample Lesson Plan	205
Appendix D.2	Lesson Plan (Blank)	206
References		208
Suggested Readings		209
About the Author		211

Series Preface

The Steps to Success Activity Series is a breakthrough in skill instruction through the development of complete learning progressions—the *steps to success*. These *steps* help students quickly perform basic skills successfully and prepare them to acquire advanced skills readily. At each step, students are encouraged to learn at their own pace and to integrate their new skills into the total action of the activity, which motivates them to achieve.

The unique features of the Steps to Success Activity Series are the result of comprehensive development—through analyzing existing activity books, incorporating the latest research from the sport sciences and consulting with students, instructors, teacher educators, and administrators. This groundwork pointed up the need for three different types of books—for participants, instructors, and teacher educators—which we have created and together comprise the Steps to Success Activity Series.

The *participant book* for each activity is a self-paced, step-by-step guide; learners can use it as a primary resource for a beginning activity class or as a self-instructional guide. The unique features of each *step* in the participant book include

- sequential illustrations that clearly show proper technique for all basic skills,
- helpful suggestions for detecting and correcting errors,
- excellent drill progressions with accompanying *Success Goals* for measuring performance, and
- a complete checklist for each basic skill for a trained observer to rate the learner's technique.

A comprehensive *instructor guide* accompanies the participant's book for each activity, emphasizing how to individualize instruction. Each *step* of the instructor's guide promotes successful teaching and learning with

- teaching cues (*Keys to Success*) that emphasize fluidity, rhythm, and wholeness,

- criterion-referenced rating charts for evaluating a participant's initial skill level,
- suggestions for observing and correcting typical errors,
- tips for group management and safety,
- ideas for adapting every drill to increase or decrease the difficulty level,
- quantitative evaluations for all drills (*Success Goals*), and
- a complete test bank of written questions.

The series textbook, *Instructional Design for Teaching Physical Activities*, explains the *steps to success* model, which is the basis for the Steps to Success Activity Series. Teacher educators can use this text in their professional preparation classes to help future teachers and coaches learn how to design effective physical activity programs in school, recreation, or community teaching and coaching settings.

After identifying the need for participant, instructor, and teacher educator texts, we refined the *steps to success* instructional design model and developed prototypes for the participant and the instructor books. Once these prototypes were fine-tuned, we carefully selected authors for the activities who were not only thoroughly familiar with their sports but had years of experience in teaching them. Each author had to be known as a gifted instructor who understands the teaching of sport so thoroughly that he or she could readily apply the *steps to success* model.

Next, all of the participant and instructor manuscripts were carefully developed to meet the guidelines of the *steps to success* model. Then our production team, along with outstanding artists, created a highly visual, user-friendly series of books.

The result: The Steps to Success Activity Series is the premier sports instructional series available today. The participant books are the best available for helping you to become a master player, the instructor guides will help you to become a master teacher, and the teacher educator's text prepares you to design your own programs.

This series would not have been possible without the contributions of the following:

- Dr. Joan Vickers, instructional design expert,
- Dr. Rainer Martens, Publisher,
- the staff of Human Kinetics Publishers, and

- the *many* students, teachers, coaches, consultants, teacher educators, specialists, and administrators who shared their ideas—and dreams.

Judy Patterson Wright
Series Editor

Preface

Teaching Tennis: Steps to Success was written for people who teach college-level tennis activity courses. This book also reflects my approach to teaching tennis to other groups, which have included high school physical education classes, beginners at racket clubs, municipal and summer program participants, and even players on tennis teams. Having worked in each of those situations, I have tried to bring that experience to you in a style that is simple, direct, and practical. The methods of teaching found in this book are being used every time I go on the court for lessons or classes, and they have been presented to tennis teachers in conferences and workshops around the country.

My primary objective in writing *Teaching Tennis: Steps to Success* is to prepare a person with a sports or physical education background to go out and teach tennis classes. However, I also wrote for those of you who have tennis teaching experience. Even though I have played, taught, and written about tennis most of my life, I learn something every time I talk with another teacher or attend another conference. In many ways, this book is a summary of all of those conversations, meetings, and experiences I have had playing, teaching, and coaching tennis.

Both the participant's book (*Tennis: Steps to Success*) and this instructor's guide have been presented in a way that combines visual and verbal approaches. If you want to scan either book for ideas, fundamental skills, corrective techniques, and drills, there are enough lists, short explanations, and illustrations to prepare you for the classroom or the tennis court without having to read every word. However, when you have the time, need, and interest to get more information, it is also there—in a way that is meant to be easy to read and easy to put into practice on the court.

You can use this book as a complete, step-by-step teaching package, or you can choose just the ideas and activities that work for you. As a teacher, I have never picked up a book that absolutely perfectly presented a program that I followed to the letter. Although I hope this book comes close to being the complete package, I really expect the reader to combine this information with his or her own knowledge and skills to produce an even more effective tennis teaching experience.

Finally, *Tennis: Steps to Success* and *Teaching Tennis: Steps to Success* establish a format that can be used in many other activity classes. Many of you teach a variety of courses. With this book and the others in this series, you can prepare, organize, teach, and evaluate each course in a way that is consistent and easy to follow. Instead of wasting time getting used to each other, you and your students will know what to expect. With that out of the way, teaching and learning can start on the first day of class and can continue on a predictable course the rest of the term.

I would like to thank Ebbie Whitten and Inez Schindler for teaching me to write, Lloyd Johnson for teaching me to play tennis, and Hans Leis for teaching me to teach tennis.

Jim Brown

Implementing the Steps to Success Staircase

This book is meant to be flexible for not only your students' needs but for your needs as well. It is common to hear that students' perceptions of a task change as the task is learned. However, it is often forgotten that teachers' perceptions and actions also change (Goc-Karp & Zakrajsek, 1987; Housner & Griffey, 1985; Imwold & Hoffman, 1983).

More experienced or master teachers tend to approach the teaching of activities in a similar manner. They are highly organized (e.g., they do not waste time getting groups together or using long explanations); they integrate information (from biomechanics, kinesiology, exercise physiology, motor learning, sport psychology, cognitive psychology, instructional design, etc.); and they relate basic skills into the larger game or performance context, succinctly explaining why the basic skills, concepts, and tactics are important within the game or performance setting. Then, usually within a few minutes, they place their students into realistic practice situations that progress the student in steps that follow logical manipulations of factors such as

- the addition or removal of equipment,
- the number of skills used in combination,
- the size and distance of targets,
- the distance between players,
- the number of people used in tactical combinations (1 vs. 0, 1 vs. 1, 1 vs. 2, and 2 vs. 2),
- the rules used, and
- the pace of the ball.

This book will show you how the basic tennis skills and selected physiological, psychological, and other pertinent knowledge are interrelated (see Appendix A for an overview). You can use this information not only to gain insights into the various interrelationships but also to define the subject matter for tennis. The following questions offer specific suggestions for implementing this knowledge base and help you evaluate and improve your teaching methods, which include class organization, drills, objectives, progressions, and evaluations.

1. Under what conditions do you teach?
   - How much space is available?
   - What type of equipment is available?
   - What is the average class size?
   - How much time is allotted per class session?
   - How many class sessions do you teach?
   - Do you have any teaching assistants?

2. What are your students' initial skill levels?
   - Look for the rating charts located in the beginning of most steps (chapters) to identify the criteria that discriminate between beginning, intermediate, and advanced skill levels.

3. What is the best order to teach tennis skills?
   - Follow the sequence of steps (chapters) used in this book.
   - See Appendix B.1 for suggestions on when to introduce, review, or continue practicing each step.
   - Based on your answers to the previous questions, use the form in Appendix B.2 to put into order the steps that you will be able to cover in the time available.

4. What objectives do you want your students to accomplish by the end of a lesson, unit, or course?
   - For your technique or qualitative objectives, select from the Student Keys to Success (or see the Keys to Success Checklists in *Tennis: Steps to Success*) that are provided for all basic skills.
   - For your performance or quantitative objectives, select from the Student Success Goals provided for each drill.

- For written questions on rules, strokes, and strategy, select from the Test Bank of written questions.
- See the Sample Individual Program (Appendix C.1) for selected technique and performance objectives for a 16-week unit.
- For unit objectives, adjust your total number of selected objectives to fit your unit length (use the form in Appendix C.2).
- See the Sample Group Program (Appendix C.3) for evaluation modifications with large groups.
- For organizing daily objectives, see the Sample Lesson Plan in Appendix D.1, and modify the basic lesson plan form in Appendix D.2 to best fit your needs.

5. How will you evaluate your students?

- Read the section ''Evaluation Ideas.''
- Decide on your type of grading system; you could use letter grades, pass-fail, total points, percentages, skill levels (bronze, silver, gold), and so forth.

6. Which activities should be selected to achieve student objectives?

- Follow the drills for each step because they are specifically designed for large groups of students and are presented in an easy-to-difficult order. Avoid a random approach to selecting drills and exercises.

- Modify drills as necessary to best fit each student's skill level by following the suggestions for decreasing and increasing the difficulty level of each drill.
- Ask your students to meet the Success Goal listed for each drill.
- Use the cross-reference to the corresponding step and drill in the participant's book, *Tennis: Steps to Success*, for class assignments or makeups. The bracketed notation [New drill] after a drill title indicates that the drill appears only in this instructor's guide and will be new to your students.

7. What rules and expectations do you have for your class?

- For general management and safety guidelines, read the section ''Class Management and Organization.''
- For specific guidelines, read the subhead ''Group Management and Safety Tips'' included with each drill.
- Let your students know what your rules are during your class orientation or first day of class. Then post the rules and discuss them often.

Teaching is a complex task, requiring you to make many decisions that affect both you and your students (see Figure 1). Use this book to create an effective and successful learning experience for you and everyone you teach. And remember, have fun too!

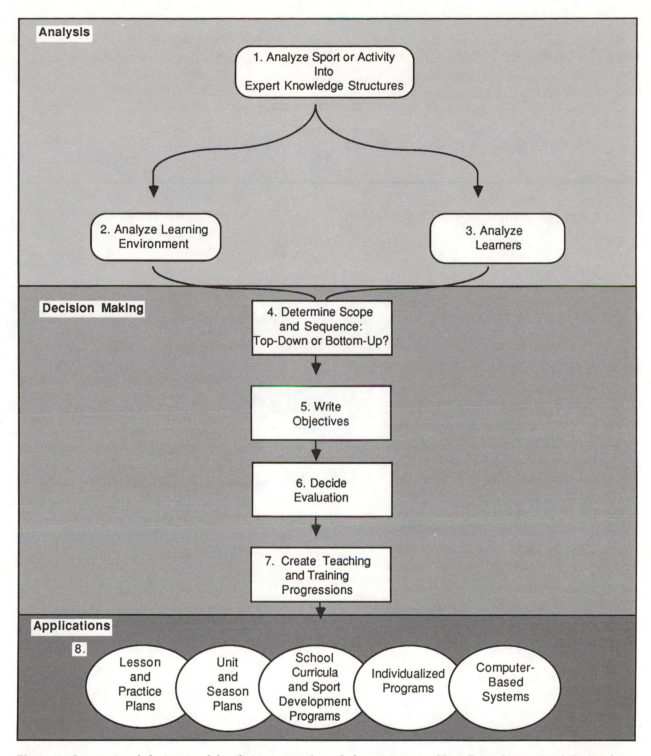

Figure 1 Instructional design model utilizing expert knowledge structures. *Note.* From *Instructional Design for Teaching Physical Activities* by J.N. Vickers, 1990, Champaign, IL: Human Kinetics. Copyright by Joan N. Vickers. Reprinted by permission. This instructional design model has appeared in earlier forms in *Badminton: A Structures of Knowledge Approach* (p. 1) by J.N. Vickers and D. Brecht, 1987, Calgary, AB: University Printing Services. Copyright 1987 by Joan N. Vickers; and "The Role of Expert Knowledge Structures in an Instructional Design Model for Physical Education" by J.N. Vickers, 1983, *Journal of Teaching in Physical Education*, **2**(3), p. 20. Copyright 1983 by Joan N. Vickers.

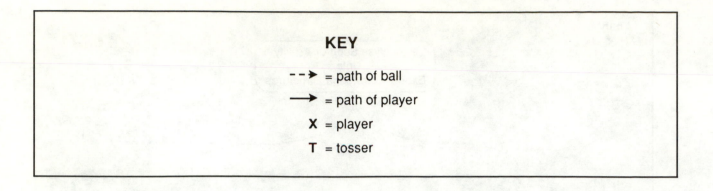

Class Management and Organization

If you know you are going to teach a tennis course, there are several areas of preparation to consider before classes begin. The kind of students has a lot to do with how you should prepare. How old are the students? How many will there be in each class? Are they physical education majors? Are the students required to take the course? Are they beginners, intermediates, advanced players, or a mixed group? With the answers to these questions, you can make good decisions about class organization and student objectives.

PRECOURSE MANAGEMENT DECISIONS

Some of the decisions that have to be made may have already been determined by school or departmental policy, tradition, or unwritten guidelines of other teachers. If this is the case, all you have to do is check with your supervisor to learn what the policies are. If not, consider the following items before the first class meeting. The purpose here is not to suggest policies but to let you know what has to be planned.

How will tennis balls and rackets be furnished, how many will be needed, and where will they be stored?
Some schools provide all the equipment for students; others require students to bring their own rackets and cans of balls. If the students bring their own balls (and mark them), time will be needed at the end of each class to retrieve and sort them. Storage can be provided by the school or be made the responsibility of the students.

How many courts are available, and have they been cleared for your use?
Check to see that there is no schedule conflict with other teachers, other departments, private groups, or varsity teams. Also check to see whether the courts are in good playing condition and what you can do if they are not.

How will students dress, and what provisions are there for storing and cleaning clothes and towels?
The alternatives for dress are (a) no special requirements, (b) gym shorts and T-shirts, and (c) school PE uniforms. As with equipment, storage can be the responsibility of the school or the students.

What are the student objectives for the course?
If not already established, objectives vary with the nature of the students. If you are asked to write objectives, they should be written in terms of observable and measurable student behavior. For example, an objective could look like this: ''The student successfully serves 5 of 10 balls using the Continental grip and a full-swing motion.'' The Success Goals in this book reflect reasonable expectations for beginners, based on years of teaching and observing activity courses.

Is there a course outline to follow?
If not, one should be developed with a scope (content) and sequence (progression of learning activities) format. This book provides both.

What will students be assigned in addition to class activities?
Written reports, magazine articles, participation in extraclass competition, attendance at tennis matches, unit plans, and field trips are possible, depending on the group taking the course.

How will students be graded?
Factors that may be considered are skill tests, written tests, written work assignments, attendance, improvement, and attitude.

What is the policy on injuries?
For a student who becomes injured and cannot participate in activities, there must be some established policy. A school may give an ''incomplete'' grade, require the student to drop the course, allow written work to replace activity, or set a maximum grade that can be attained without full participation.

What is the policy on absences?
Develop a routine for checking class attendance. Students may be seated in bleachers near the courts, asked to stand next to a fence or wall on numbers or in spaces, or they may be assigned to courts. If students are absent make it very clear to them at the beginning of a semester or school year what the rules are concerning classes missed. Some schools allow a predetermined number of absences without penalty, some have no policy, and others leave it to individual instructors to determine their own rules. In activity courses, it is an accepted practice to grade on participation—that is, attendance—as well as on fundamental skills, overall play, and written work. Whatever system is to be used, make class attendance necessary in order to pass the course.

How will the class be taught on bad-weather days?
Make sure there is a place for your class to meet indoors. Prepare some classroom presentations in advance, such as rules discussions, films, videotapes, gymnasium routines, exercise sessions, reports on magazine articles, and question-and-answer contests. See the ''Gymnasium and Classroom Activities'' section in this book for specific instructions.

ON-COURT MANAGEMENT

Following are some suggestions for organizing classes so that they will be interesting, productive, appropriately paced, and enjoyable. Above all, remember that you are teaching an activity course—not a lecture course.

Make sure that there is more actual hitting than talking by you and your students. Once your students are on the court, they should be either hitting, tossing, or picking up balls almost all of the time. Keep their standing in line at a minimum.

Getting Classes Started

- Make players responsible for helping move ball baskets and other equipment to and from the court before and after classes.

- Start classes with activities in which no one stands in line. Use warm-ups, racket-handling drills, or serving drills, for example.
- Try to start every class with an activity in which no one has to pick up tennis balls; beginning a class by having to pick up balls is no fun.
- Keep explanations brief, 30 seconds or less. The sooner students begin hitting, the sooner they begin to learn.
- Use a centrally located court for explanations and demonstrations, instead of having all players meet at Court 1 then make a time-consuming trip back to the far courts.
- Do not assume that students understand your tennis terminology. Check to see what they think you mean.
- Place weaker players with the wind at their backs, giving them the advantage of the extra power the wind provides.

Conducting Drills

- Occasionally mix strong and weak players on the same court in drills in which they do not have to hit against each other.
- When students are conducting the same drill on multiple courts, align players exactly in the same formation on every court. This way you can look down a series of courts and see the same skill being practiced throughout your field of vision.
- Suggest corrections as soon as you see errors. If you don't, by the time you get to the court where the correction needs to be made, other shots will have been hit, and the critical teaching moment will have been lost.
- Use as many low-key, fun games and activities as possible with young players, as opposed to straight hitting drills. Inexperienced players need to have some success other than playing games and sets. These players are simply not ready for match competition, so invent ways for them to be successful and to have fun. Older, more serious players can concentrate on the task of learning strokes more

easily without the added incentives of games and activities.

- Alternate vigorous drills with ones in which students only stand and hit.
- Rotate players so that no one gets stuck on a court where he or she is not comfortable with the other players.
- In accuracy drills, use targets large enough to ensure that players will hit them (boxes or ball baskets, for example).
- Position ball feeders close to the net to increase the number of hits in a given period of time. Feeders placed at the baseline can feed only about half as many shots per minute as those closer to the net.
- Spend some time on agility and throwing skills with beginning groups.
- Although there will be exceptions, weaker players and groups respond better to positive reinforcement than to critical remarks. As players become more sophisticated and secure in their games, they need less emotional stroking and more direct, helpful advice.
- Set individual goals when possible and measure students' progress on such skills as putting balls into play, serves, and consecutive groundstrokes and volleys.

Picking Up Balls

- Use as many tennis balls per court as possible. A minimum of 3 balls per pair of players is absolutely necessary. In ideal situations, 150 balls per court is not too many.
- Have one or two players at a time pick up balls to keep action continuous, but be sure they do it out of the line of balls being hit.
- When the balls are so scattered that everyone has to stop and pick them up, they should bump balls to the net or to the fence, then take the baskets to where the balls are. Allowing students to move around the court picking up balls one at a time consumes too much time.
- Place baskets of balls against the fence or the wall during serving drills to avoid players getting hit with backswings.

- Take time to clear the court of tennis balls during drills. Stepping on balls twists ankles, which is a frequent injury in group instruction.

Finishing Classes

- Finish classes with vigorous, demanding drills or activities.
- Name a player of the day and reward that player with recognition, an inexpensive prize, or a special privilege (like not having to pick up balls at the end of the class).
- With children's groups, give racket stickers or other rewards for good attendance, outstanding shots, reaching goals, best ball picker-upper, and so on.
- Give students time to cool down and clean up before the next class.

NINE LEGAL DUTIES

Lawsuits are increasing at an alarming rate. As the number of people taking tennis and other activity courses grows, the potential for violations of safety practices, for injuries, and for lawsuits increases even more. In order to protect your students and yourself, consider the following guidelines:

1. Adequate Supervision

Provide adequate supervision. This means that you should be present at the court when classes or practice sessions are being conducted. Sending a message for the class to get started without you or leaving a class before the time has expired is an invitation to legal trouble. If you cannot attend a class, make sure that a school-approved substitute is present. Specific supervision also means that you should be in a position to start, conduct, and stop each class activity. Standing in a position to see as many students as possible at the same time must be balanced with the time given to individual students for instruction.

2. Sound Planning

Give your students the benefit of good, sound planning. Gradual, cumulative progression is essential; plan your skill instruction, practices, and drills so that your players do not move too rapidly into techniques or contests beyond their skill levels. Improvement should be a goal, but this improvement should be consistent with readiness factors. Plan a sequence of activities that students can reasonably be expected to perform. Both the participant's book and this instructor's book have been designed to introduce skills at the appropriate time and to follow a steady learning progression throughout the course.

Take physical skills, physical condition, weather conditions, court conditions, and time allotment into consideration when planning lessons. You will be limited in the variety of drills for beginners because they do not have the skills for the rapid exchange of a variety of shots. For example, beginners cannot perform well in a rapid-fire volley drill. As these players develop, they can be expected to accomplish more, and you can use a wider range of class activities.

Beginners cannot demonstrate endurance as well as experienced players; they do better in shorter time periods than extended ones. All players have difficulty working in high temperature and humidity. Having access to water at the courts is essential to their health and your peace of mind.

The primary court problem tennis teachers encounter is not enough room. At the college level, work with the administration to limit the number of students per court. Four players per court is reasonable; anything higher can present safety problems and will challenge your ability to keep students actively involved.

Push your students toward excellence but use sound, safe educational planning to reach your teaching goals. The amount of time allotted for most activity courses is not sufficient to master tennis skills. In 1-hour courses, students are usually given 10 minutes to dress out and 10 minutes to dress in, leaving 40 minutes for learning. Fifty-minute classes are not unusual at the high school and college levels, giving 10 minutes less instruction. Tuesday–Thursday classes of 1 hour or more actual court time seem to work better for most activity courses.

Teachers who use sound planning will be effective under almost any conditions.

3. Inherent Risks

Warn your players of risks inherent in tennis and of the dangers of using questionable techniques. Such risks in tennis are presented by vigorous exercise affecting the respiratory, muscular, skeletal, and cardiovascular systems, as well as safety risks of being hit by rackets, balls, and other people on the same court. Questionable techniques include incorrect grips and trying to hit the ball too hard over a period of time. Repeat these warnings sufficiently so that your players know, understand, and appreciate the risks they may encounter.

Although a waiver-of-rights form is used in some schools and clubs, these documents have not been upheld in most court cases: Students cannot waive their rights. They may sign a consent form acknowledging the inherent risks of an activity, but even this will not hold up in a trial if negligence on the part of the institution can be proved. Some of the most common injuries associated with tennis include being struck in the eye with a ball that glances off the racket frame, stepping on a ball and twisting an ankle, slipping and falling on the court, and being hit with a racket (either the player's own racket or someone else's). Players with cardiovascular and respiratory problems should be warned about activities that may complicate these conditions. In areas of high temperatures and humidity, students should be warned of such problems as dehydration, heat exhaustion, and overexposure to the sun.

4. Safe Playing Environment

Provide a safe environment for practice and play. This requires not just safe tennis courts and gymnasium but also properly used equipment. It is your responsibility to inspect your facility and equipment regularly and thoroughly. Damp, wet, or slick courts are a problem every tennis teacher faces. During bad weather, decisions have to be made whether to conduct classes on such potentially dangerous surfaces. Test the surface yourself if you are in doubt.

A second problem in large classes is players' being hit by tennis balls from another court or another player. It is imperative that when you give instructions for a drill or activity to stop, everyone hears the command and obeys it. When a few players decide to get in a couple of extra shots while others are moving to pick up balls or change courts, the probability of an injury is very high. Take strong action to prevent this kind of accident. Reprimand or punish those who do not follow your instructions.

5. Evaluating Students' Disabilities

Evaluate your students for injuries or incapacities; determine whether any limitations on participation are appropriate. Your institution may have policies already established in this area, and it is your duty to know what these policies are. If there is no policy, develop your own for your classes. A questionnaire could be developed to provide you with information about your students' physical and emotional health, but care should be taken not to invade their right to privacy. A common-sense approach would be to announce to the entire class that if anyone has a physical or emotional problem that you, the teacher, should know about, that person should privately advise you of the problem. Then you can plan lessons accordingly and avoid the possibility of an injury or illness.

6. Matching Opponents

Match, or equate, students for practice and competitive conditions. Failing to properly match participants has resulted in legal verdicts of negligence on the part of the teacher. Matching is more important in contact sports than in tennis from a legal perspective. Still, grouping players by ability makes drills, activities, and competition more productive. The tennis accident most likely to occur because of unequal ability among players on the same court is for the least experienced player to get hit by a hard-hit ball.

7. Emergency First Aid Procedures

Provide proper first aid equipment and establish emergency medical procedures that can be put into action immediately. A well-stocked first aid kit should at least be located where you can get to it quickly, if it is not actually with you on the courts. The items most likely to be needed are Band-aids®, bandages, elastic wraps, and ice (or chemical cold-packs).

8. Student Civil Rights

Your students' civil rights follow them onto the tennis court. Our judicial system requires you to assure that the basic rights of your students are not violated. It is no longer as easy for you to place restrictions on the appearance or expression of your students, but appropriate dress and behavior can still be expected and enforced. In the event of a dispute, follow the basic principles of due process. Every school should have a system to see that teachers and students are given an opportunity to have their sides of the story heard.

9. General Legal Concerns

Be knowledgeable of guidelines concerning transportation and insurance. This is especially true if personal vehicles are used to move students to and from tennis courts, classrooms, and dressing areas.

Sports lawsuits can involve large amounts of money and can financially ruin a teacher or coach. Therefore, it is a good idea to carry adequate personal liability insurance. You can purchase large amounts of personal liability insurance at reasonable rates from a variety of sources.

Finally, keep good records, particularly in the event of an injury. Report every injury to the proper authorities as soon after the incident as possible. Fill out the right forms, make copies for yourself, and see that the papers get to the right administrators at your school. In all potentially troublesome situations, make notes while the events are still clear in your mind. Do not trust your memory for details of events that may turn out to have occurred months or years prior to a deposition, hearing, or trial.

CLASS WARM-UPS

The participant's book, *Tennis: Steps to Success*, describes specifically tennis-related warm-up exercises. Encourage your students to use those exercises and to be ready for drills, activities, and play when the class period begins. For students who do not have time for preclass warm-ups and for instructors who prefer to conduct a group warm-up routine, some exercises follow. All of the stretching exercises in Activities 3 through 9 can be performed with the same class formation, which we will call the *standard class warm-up formation*. In this formation, spread players evenly along the baselines and service lines on both sides of the net and facing the net. They need room to stretch and swing rackets without hitting anyone. Group leaders can stand near the net so they can be seen by players on both sides of the net. This formation is described further in Warm-Up 3.

1. Court Jog
(up to 16 players per court)

Students start at the baselines facing the net, 3 to 4 feet apart, with rackets in hand (Diagram WF.1). At your command to go, the students jog (a) forward to the service line; (b) backward to the baseline, still facing the net; (c) forward and touch the net with the racket; and (d) backward to the baseline. They carry the racket in the ready position and face the net while jogging. Let them rest for 15 seconds, then repeat the routine.

2. Side to Side
(up to 16 players)

Students start at the center service line (and extended center service line), 3 to 4 feet apart, with rackets in hand (Diagram WF.2). At your command to go, the students use shuffle steps to move (a) to the right singles sideline, (b) back across the center line, (c) to the right doubles sideline, and (d) back to the starting position. Let them rest 15 seconds, then repeat the routine, but having them move to the left sideline first.

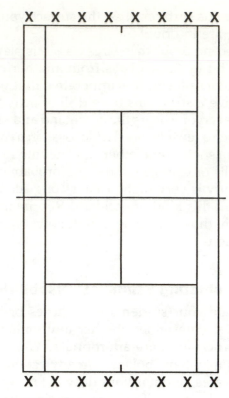

Diagram WF.1 Court jog.

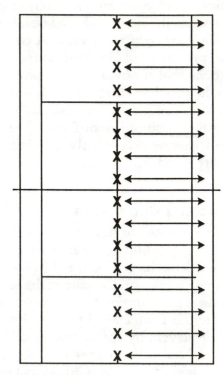

Diagram WF.2 Side to side.

3. Neck Stretch
(up to 40 players per court)

Students take positions along the baseline, service line, and imaginary lines behind the baseline and service line, 3 to 4 feet apart, and facing the net. On their own, students hold their heads and necks upright and turn them alternately to the right and left sides 10 times (Diagram WF.3).

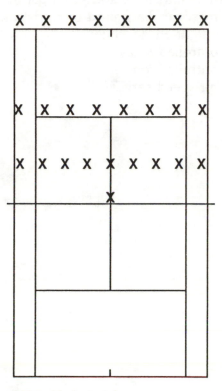

Diagram WF.3 Neck stretch.

4. Upper-Body Rotation
(up to 40 players per court)

Using the standard class warm-up formation described in the previous warm-up, the students clasp their own hands together in front of their chests and rotate their upper bodies back and forth to the right and left, 10 times each, trying not to rotate their hips.

5. Achilles Stretch
(up to 40 players per court)

Using the standard class warm-up formation, the students put left feet forward. The students lean forward and down with both feet pointing straight to stretch the Achilles tendon. They should not bounce. They do this 5 times, then lean forward on the other foot 5 times.

6. Groin Stretch
(up to 40 players per court)

Using the standard class warm-up formation, the students again lean forward and down, but point the front foot forward and the back one to the side. They should not bounce. They do this 5 times, then lean forward on the other foot.

7. Lower Back and Hamstring Stretch
(up to 40 players per court)

Using the standard class warm-up formation, the students stand with their legs straight and their feet together. They reach to grasp their legs as low as possible. They should not bounce. They hold this stretch for 5 seconds.

8. Service Stretch
(up to 40 players per court)

Using the standard class warm-up formation, the students swing through the service motion 10 times with (or without) the racket cover on the racket.

9. Shoulder Stretch
(up to 40 players per court)

Using the standard class warm-up formation, students hold their rackets at both ends and reach back as far as possible. They do this 5 times.

10. Hitting Exercises
(up to 6 players per court)

Warming up by hitting presents a problem. Beginners want to hit but have not been taught enough fundamental skills to keep the ball in play. Intermediate and advanced players are capable of warming up with rallies on the court, using the proper technique. Consequently, there are at least two levels of players in most classes, and both may want an on-court warm-up period.

One way to avoid problems is to be there to direct traffic and match players when the students arrive at the courts. Encourage beginning players to use some of the warm-up techniques other than hitting. As they develop their skills, they can begin the following hitting routines, staying in the forecourt area. Intermediate and advanced players can hit groundstrokes from the baseline and volleys at the net. They may practice any combination of the following strokes, stressing control and technique, not power. However, do not let students compete during the warm-up. Have them get loose, keeping the ball and their bodies under control and hitting shots that allow the practice partner to warm up, also. Here are some commonly used warm-up hitting routines:

- Down-the-middle groundstrokes
- Down-the-line groundstrokes
- Crosscourt forehand groundstrokes
- Crosscourt backhand groundstrokes
- Straight-ahead volleys
- Controlled smashes
- Controlled lobs
- Half-speed serves

Step 1   Handling the Racket

Learning to handle the racket is obviously a skill only beginners need to practice; intermediate and advanced players in your classes and groups can spend racket-handling time on more complex tennis skills. For beginners and, especially, younger players, time should be spent at the start of most lessons getting used to the racket and the things it can do. You will immediately know which players should and should not be doing the following drills: The students who are not challenged by the drills don't need them; the players who struggle to dribble the ball with the racket, to stop the ball with the strings, or to hold the racket properly should first master these relatively simple skills. Which activities and drills they use are not as important as the fact that students are doing something with their rackets. Players can invent their own racket-handling tricks as well as learn the ones suggested by you.

Make racket-handling activities fun for students. Although the following introductory drills build fundamental racket skills, they can be tedious and boring unless used creatively. Racket-handling skills also give students an opportunity to begin a class actively while you are getting organized and late students are arriving at the courts. Allow those who are there on time to use the first 5 minutes productively and enjoyably.

STUDENT KEYS TO SUCCESS

- Use a forehand grip
- Keep arm extended
- Don't overswing or overhit

Racket-Handling Rating

CHECKPOINT	BEGINNING LEVEL	INTERMEDIATE LEVEL	ADVANCED LEVEL
Grip	• Does not remember grip described • Uses Western grip frequently • Chokes up on racket • Has trouble changing grips	• Not applicable	• Not applicable
Ball Control	• No concept of hard and soft hits • Misses, or hits frame • Ball gets too close to body		

Racket-Handling Rating

CHECKPOINT	BEGINNING LEVEL	INTERMEDIATE LEVEL	ADVANCED LEVEL
Movement	• Jerky, lunging • Gets in others' way • Cannot move and keep ball under control		

Error Detection and Correction for Racket Handling

Remember that the focus of racket-handling activities—at least at this stage of learning—is for students to get used to holding the racket, maneuvering it, and controlling the ball with it. Do not overteach beginners struggling with their rackets; tell them or show them just enough to help them get through the simple drills. This may mean showing them how to hold a forehand grip without going into detail. It does not mean that you have to show them the backhand grip, unless you add racket-handling drills using that grip. Getting students through the simple drills could also involve suggestions about how to extend their arms or to move their feet, but this should not be the time to have them worrying about too many details. There will be plenty of time later for more sophisticated teaching and learning.

ERROR ⊘ **CORRECTION**

1. Student uses an incorrect grip (especially the Western grip).

1. Demonstrate the Eastern forehand repeatedly. Mark a spot on the player's wrist as point of reference between the racket handle and the hand. Use an elastic bandage to tie the racket and hand position.

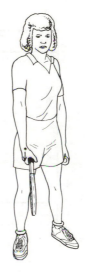

2. Student has poor ball control.

2. Use best players to practice bumps with beginners. Insist on soft, low "ups" and "downs." Allow choking up if necessary. Let student practice bumping with hand instead of racket.

3. Student makes jerky movements.

3. Have student practice stationary activities until skill improves. Have student use graduated hitting and moving progressions. Physically hold racket with student.

Racket-Handling Drills

1. Ups and Downs
[Corresponds to *Tennis*, Step 1, Drills 2 and 3]

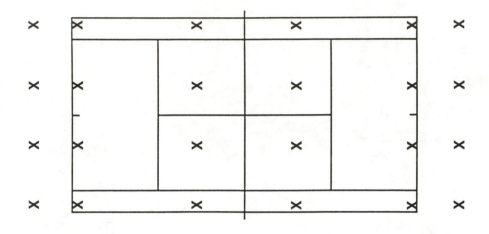

Group Management and Safety Tips
- Spread students on court for room to maneuver.
- Allow 2 to 5 minutes of practice.
- Suggest variations (such as hitting the ball with the racket edges) for students who finish sooner than others.

Equipment
- Rackets, 1 per student
- Balls, 1 per student

Instructions to Class
- "Hold the racket with a forehand grip and practice dribbling the ball on the court. Let the ball come up to your strings before moving the racket down for another dribble. Now turn your palm up and practice air dribbles. Keep the ball under control by bumping it a few inches into the air."

Student Option
- "Set your own goal for the number of repetitions."

Student Success Goal
- 50 dribbles down and 50 bounces up in 5 minutes

To Decrease Difficulty
- Show student how to choke up on racket handle.
- Tell student to let the ball bounce on the ground between "ups."
- Reduce the Success Goal to 45 or 40.

To Increase Difficulty
- Have student alternate ups and downs.
- Have student alternate shots with partner.
- Increase the Success Goal by increments of 5.

2. Line Bumps

[Corresponds to *Tennis*, Step 1, Drill 6, *Variation*]

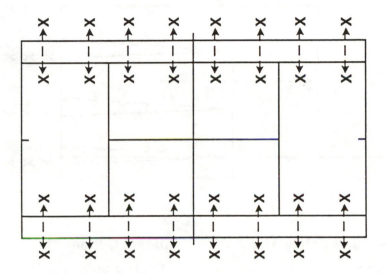

Group Management and Safety Tips

- Match players according to ability.
- Place 4 to 5 pairs in each of the 4 alley areas.
- Rotate partners every minute for variety.
- Allow 3 to 4 minutes for the drill.

Equipment

- Rackets, 1 per student
- Balls, 3 per student pair

Instructions to Class

- "With a partner, place a ball on each line of a doubles alley. Stand opposite each other, two steps 'behind' the lines. Now bump a third ball back and forth, trying to hit your partner's ball. Let the strings do the work. Don't try to hit the ball hard."

Student Option

- "Keep score either by counting balls that hit in the alley or by counting those that make a direct hit on the ball."

Student Success Goal

- Bump partner's ball at least once.

To Decrease Difficulty

- Have student choke up on the racket.
- Have student play with you or a stronger player.
- Just make student hit 10 consecutive shots instead of having to bump partner's ball.

To Increase Difficulty

- Increase the distance student must stand from line.
- Rule that points are lost with shots hit beyond lines.
- Require two target hits before drill ends.

3. *Dribble Relay*
[New drill]

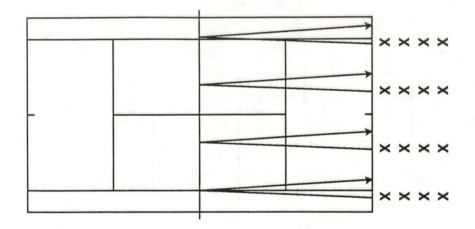

Group Management and Safety Tips

- Balance the teams.
- Place extra balls at the net in case some players lose control.
- Demonstrate slanting the racket forward to prevent getting too close to the ball.
- This is one drill where good technique increases speed also.

Equipment

- Balls, 1 per team
- Rackets, 1 per student

Instructions to Class

- "Form four teams. Equal numbers of players stand single-file behind the baseline, facing the net. The first player in each line dribbles the ball forward until reaching the net, then dribbles back and gives the ball to the next player in line. Keep the ball out in front of your position. Dribble it where you are going to be, not where you are. The first team to have every player dribble to the net and back wins."

Student Option

- "You may dribble the ball in the air instead of bouncing it on the court."

Student Success Goals

- Participate in at least one race.
- Complete the course without losing control of the ball.

To Decrease Difficulty

- Start teams at the service line instead of the baseline.
- Have each student dribble ball alone instead of as part of a team.
- Repeat the drill without competition; students should concentrate on technique rather than speed.

To Increase Difficulty

- Make student run and dribble instead of going at own pace.
- Have student return to the starting line after any mistake. This introduces the idea of performing under pressure and being penalized for mistakes.

4. Racket Routine
[New drill]

Group Management and Safety Tips

- Allow 5 minutes for students to develop routines.
- Spectators or students not dressed out serve as judges.
- Allow each team to announce a team name.
- Allow a group one-half of a court to perform on, while all other groups watch from other half.
- Reward winners, if possible.

Equipment

- Rackets, 1 per student
- Balls, 1 per student
- Tape recorder and tapes, if music is used

Instructions to Class

- "Divide into groups of four to six players. Take 5 minutes to create and practice a team racket-handling routine. Be creative. Here are some possible routines to practice: alternating ups and downs; alternating ups, downs, and bouncing the ball on the racket edge; dribbling the ball behind your back or between your legs; using the racket to pick balls up off the court in three different ways; performing ups or downs to music; using a combination of tricks with a partner; catching the ball in the air with your racket strings. Each group will perform its routine in front of the class for 1 minute. The winning team does not have to pick up balls after the first drill."

Student Option

- "You can increase your chance of winning by attempting more difficult routines."

Student Success Goal

- Create one trick no other group can perform.

To Decrease Difficulty

- Ask teams to use only skills already practiced in class.
- Let teams perform routines in slow motion.

To Increase Difficulty

- Require performance of specific routines (see "Instructions" for examples).

Step 2 Preparing to Hit

Even though there may be beginners who move well on the tennis court and advanced players who have trouble covering the court, there is usually a relationship between shot preparation and ability level. Most beginners will not have a concept of the ready position or why it is important. Intermediates tend to hit shots very well from a stationary position but may have problems moving and hitting. Advanced players should be able to prepare well for any shot, moving well and hitting good shots from any place on the court.

Good tennis players, like most other good athletes, must have good footwork, which does not come naturally for most players. Before actual tennis movement skills can be taught, many beginning players must learn to move, period. Some of these players will not appreciate the time and work needed to develop movement skills. Some of the following drills will not have an obvious relationship to tennis movement skills. It is your job as instructor to overcome such obstacles and to present movement information and activities in a way that will help the learner, even if he or she sees no need for help in this area.

STUDENT KEYS TO SUCCESS

- Always be ready
- Anticipate shots
- Use shuffle and cross-step
- Run, plant, step, swing
- Recover quickly

Preparing to Hit Rating

CHECKPOINT	BEGINNING LEVEL	INTERMEDIATE LEVEL	ADVANCED LEVEL
Preparation	• Holds incorrect grip • Does not return to the ready position • Crowds the ball	• Changes from forehand to backhand grips • Understands the importance of the ready position	• Starts preparation immediately after previous shot • Does not have to think about grip changes
Movement	• Appears to be uncoordinated • May be off balance when hitting • Does not time movement with pace of shots	• Moves into position quickly • May have trouble hitting on the run • Frequently hits off the wrong foot	• May bounce to get body into motion • Moves easily • Looks comfortable hitting • Works hard between shots • Moves to a central position in anticipation of the next shot

Error Detection and Correction for Preparing to Hit

Focus on the feet as you watch players move. Stop drills and activities to make corrections. Have students imitate your footwork, if necessary; sometimes they can follow the leader better than follow directions.

ERROR   **CORRECTION**

1. Student hits late.

1. Tell student not to wait for the ball to bounce before starting racket preparation.

ERROR 🚫

CORRECTION

2. Student crowds the ball.

2. Tell student not to overrun the ball but to keep it at arm's length.

3. Student hits off the wrong foot.

3. Have student start moving sooner, then plant the back foot and step in the direction of the target.

ERROR   **CORRECTION**

4. Student leaves part of the court open.

4. As soon as student hits one shot, he or she should move to cover the unprotected area on the next, not wait to see where that return is going.

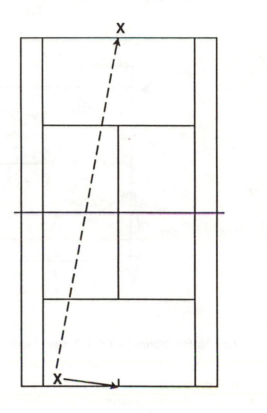

1. *Grounder Drill*
[Corresponds to *Tennis*, Step 2, Drill 1]

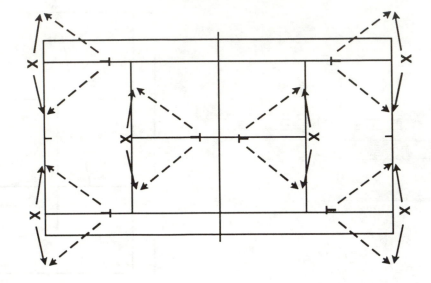

Group Management and Safety Tips

- Pair off up to 12 players and use the entire court.
- Place a tosser facing the baseline, on his or her knees or in a sitting position. Use other intersections for other pairs.
- Have spare balls available in case some are missed or returned wildly.
- Instruct fielders to bend more at the knees than at the waist.
- Be careful not to work players too hard at the beginning of a class.

Equipment

- Balls, 2 per student pair

Instructions to Class

- "Stand 12 feet from a partner, who alternates rolling balls to your right and left sides. Move to the right side, field one ball, roll it back to your partner, then move to the left to field the second. Continue the sequence for 10 balls to each side. Move without crossing your feet. Bend at the knees, not at the waist."

Student Option

- "Use the cross-step to move right and left."

Student Success Goal

- Perform the drill for 45 seconds.

To Decrease Difficulty

- Tell the tosser to decrease the side-to-side range of grounders.
- Decrease the Success Goal by 5-second increments.

To Increase Difficulty

- Tell the tosser to increase the speed and the range of the grounders.
- Increase the Success Goal by 5-second increments.

2. Wave Drill
[Corresponds to *Tennis*, Step 2, Drill 3]

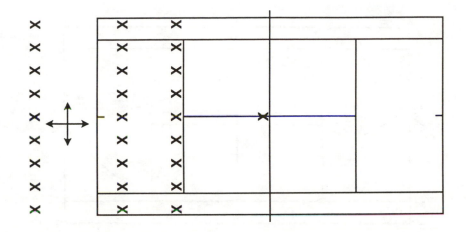

Group Management and Safety Tips
- Place students far enough apart to avoid accidental contact.
- Stand in front of the group and have them follow your lead during the first few repetitions.

Equipment
- Rackets, 1 per student

Instructions to Class
- ''Take a position on the service line or the baseline. Move forward, backward, right, and left at my signals. Carry your racket in the ready position and use the shuffle step when moving side to side. Keep your head up and look straight ahead.''

Student Option
- ''Work on your own with a partner and increase the time goal daily.''

Student Success Goal
- Perform the drill for 25 seconds.

To Decrease Difficulty
- Reduce the range of movement.
- Reduce the Success Goal by 5-second increments.

To Increase Difficulty
- Signal changes of direction more frequently.
- Increase the Success Goal by 5-second increments.

3. Fly Drill
[Corresponds to *Tennis*, Step 2, Drill 5]

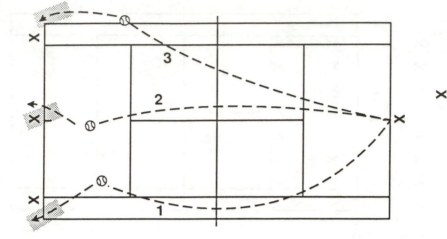

Group Management and Safety Tips

- One hitter can feed shots to three players spaced along the same baseline.
- With three players catching "flies," the hitter should alternate shots to the player in the forehand corner, then to the center, and finally to the player in the backhand corner.
- Have catchers return balls with an overhand throwing motion.
- Use a fourth player standing to the side of the hitter to retrieve balls being returned. The hitter can feed shots more quickly if not worrying about catching return throws.

Equipment

- Rackets, 1 per hitter
- Balls, 3 per student pair

Instructions to Class

- "Start without a racket at the center of your baseline. Have a partner toss or hit a series of shots from the opposite court baseline. Move to catch balls with your racket hand after one bounce. Watch the ball leave the hitter's racket and follow it all the way to your hands. Move to where the ball will come down after the bounce—not to where it will bounce."

Student Option

- "Compete against your practice partner for the higher number of consecutive catches."

Student Success Goal

- 10 consecutive catches

To Decrease Difficulty

- Instruct hitter to hit soft, easy shots.
- Allow student to let ball bounce twice before catching it.
- Allow student to make a circle in front of body with arms (hands clasped); instead of ball being caught, it bounces through the circle.

To Increase Difficulty

- Require the catcher to cover the entire court instead of sharing it with two others.
- Have hitter feed balls with more pace and lower bounces.

4. Toss Tag Drill
[Corresponds to *Tennis*, Step 2, Drill 9]

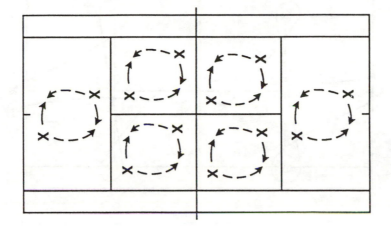

Group Management and Safety Tips

- Place at least eight players on each court at a time.
- Use four other students to act as umpires, one for each pair of players.
- Use each backcourt area for four additional players, if you need the room.

Equipment

- Balls, 1 per student pair

Instructions to Class

- "Two players take positions in a service box. One of you tosses a ball softly anywhere within the boundaries of the box so that it bounces away from your opponent, waist-high and would stay inside the box. The other player moves to catch the ball, then immediately tosses it anywhere else in the box. Win points by making your opponent miss a catch."

Student Option

- "Choose whether to make one-handed or two-handed catches."

Student Success Goal

- 10 consecutive catches

To Decrease Difficulty

- Require higher bounces.
- Reduce the Success Goal to 8 or 6.

To Increase Difficulty

- Allow lower bounces.
- Have players compete against each other for rewards.

5. Diamond Drill
[New drill]

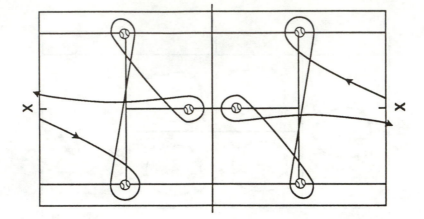

Group Management and Safety Tips

- Set individual goals.
- Show times privately to students, rather than call them out in front of the whole class.
- Use both ends of the court if additional watches are available.

Equipment

- Balls, 6
- Stopwatches, 2

Instructions to Class

- "Start at the center mark behind the baseline. Run forward and to the right to circle the ball placed at the sideline T. Move across the court to circle the ball placed at the opposite sideline T. Next, circle the ball placed a yard from the net at the center. Finally, sprint past the baseline at the center mark. It is not necessary to face the net while running."

Student Option

- "Compete against classmates for the best time."

Student Success Goal

- Establish a time and improve on it.

To Decrease Difficulty

- Have student concentrate on movement skills rather than time.

To Increase Difficulty

- Have students compete individually or as teams for best times.

6. *Footwork Drill*
[New drill]

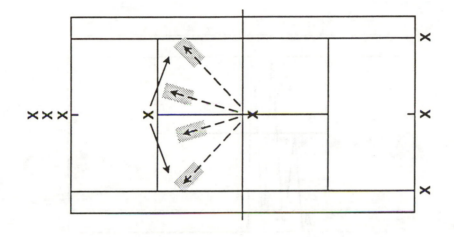

Group Management and Safety Tips
- Use this drill to finish class periods.
- Emphasize footwork and movement rather than the strokes.
- Encourage short backswings and soft hits.

Equipment
- Rackets, 1 per student pair
- Balls, 1 basket per student pair

Instructions to Class
- "Take a position at the center of the service line opposite a partner, who will toss balls anywhere in your service courts from a sitting position at the net. Return as many balls as possible during a 30-second period with the forehand. Even though some tosses will go to your backhand side, try to hit them with a forehand. The idea is to make you move your feet, regardless of where the ball goes. Later we will let you hit backhands, as well as forehands."

Student Option
- "Work with a partner on your own, increasing the Success Goal."

Student Success Goal
- Return at least half the balls to the opposite singles court with the forehand.

To Decrease Difficulty
- Reduce the drill time by 5-second increments.
- Have tosser reduce the range of balls.
- Most shots can be tossed to the forehand side instead of making the beginning player run around the backhand.

To Increase Difficulty
- Increase the drill time by 5-second increments.
- Have tosser increase the range of balls.
- More shots can be tossed to the backhand side, forcing the hitter to move extremely fast to get into a position to hit the forehand.

7. *Run the Lines*
[New drill]

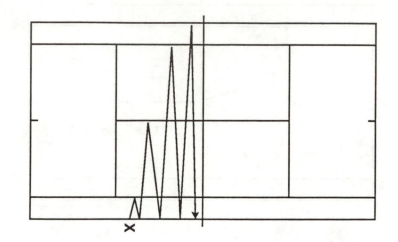

Group Management and Safety Tips

- Use this conditioning drill at the end of class periods. Remember that now the students are running, not just jogging; this is why the drill is placed at this position in the sequence of activities. Running at this pace earlier in a class might tire the students too much for them to be effective in other activities.
- Establish times, then set individual goals for each student.

Equipment

- Rackets, 1 per player
- Stopwatch

Instructions to Class

- "Line up on the doubles sideline, facing the court. On "go," run forward, touch the singles sideline with your racket, and run backward to the starting point. Then run forward to the center line and back. Run to the other singles sideline and back. Finally, run to the opposite doubles sideline and back. Face in the same direction at all times."

Student Option

- "Compete with a partner or against the clock for best times."

Student Success Goal

- Establish a time, then improve upon it.

To Decrease Difficulty

- Reduce the number of lines to be touched.

To Increase Difficulty

- Require student to cross the line with both feet instead of touching with the racket.
- Allow pairs or trios of students to compete as teams against other groups in the class. Keep cumulative times for each group.

Step 3 Groundstrokes: Forehand and Backhand

Beginning players usually fall into three groups when they start hitting groundstrokes. Some will be able to make contact and look pretty good doing it. Others struggle a little, look awkward, and have no idea where the ball is going, but make contact consistently and at least send the ball somewhere. The students in the third group struggle a lot, may even miss the ball completely, and look like hopeless cases.

You should help the first group, but don't overteach them. They may do just fine on their own. Direct most of your time toward the second group. They look out of place now, but with good teaching and practice, they will become respectable tennis players. Don't give up on the third group. You cannot let these students dominate your time and effort at the expense of the rest of the class, but most of them will eventually reach a level where they can enjoy the game. Some of them will fool you and themselves and become good players.

FOREHAND

For most players, the forehand becomes the dominant, point-winning stroke in their repertoires. See that beginners get plenty of time to develop a forehand shot with good technique. It will give them confidence, at least one shot they can count on to get in the court, and a foundation on which to build their games. When things go bad with other strokes, get them back to the forehand for a while to rebuild their confidence and consistency.

STUDENT KEYS TO SUCCESS

- Move into position quickly
- Plant back foot
- Step toward target
- Hit through ball
- Recover for next shot

Forehand Rating

CHECKPOINT	BEGINNING LEVEL	INTERMEDIATE LEVEL	ADVANCED LEVEL
Preparation	• Not in ready position • Always late • Feet in wrong position • No concept of racket position • Off balance	• Gets racket back early • Extends arm on backswing • Has a sense of racket position • Somewhat balanced	• Moves into position easily • Can judge bounces • Focuses on ball • Feet positioned for weight transfer

Forehand Rating

CHECKPOINT	BEGINNING LEVEL	INTERMEDIATE LEVEL	ADVANCED LEVEL
Swing	• Uneven swing • Erratic contact • Tucked elbow • Contact comes at varying points • Hits in front of face instead of at side • Racket turns in hand	• Develops own style • Can keep ball in play on setups • No depth on shots • Point of contact more consistent	• Has depth and control • Can hit when in trouble • Can run and hit • Uses spin • Can play against variety of styles
Follow-Through	• Racket stops with contact • No recovery for next shot	• Smooth, flowing swing • May pause before recovery	• Continues motion • Racket position varies with stroke • Quick recovery to ready position

Error Detection and Correction for the Forehand

There are at least 20 possible errors on the forehand alone. While it is important that you know what to look for, it is more important that you do not try to correct every little stroke flaw. Concentrate on major problems. Do not overload your students with information that is not essential at the moment.

ERROR

CORRECTION

1. Student has a tucked elbow through-out the swing.

1. Have student reach to hit and try hit-ting with tip end of racket. Student should start the stroke with the arm close to the body but should make contact with the arm at least partially extended.

2. Student has a floppy wrist.

2. Student should hold the wrist with the other hand and swing through 50 fore-hands, hitting this way until the rigid feeling in the wrist seems normal.

ERROR 🚫

CORRECTION

3. Student uses excessive backswing.

3. Stand behind the student and touch his or her racket with your own when it reaches the proper position.

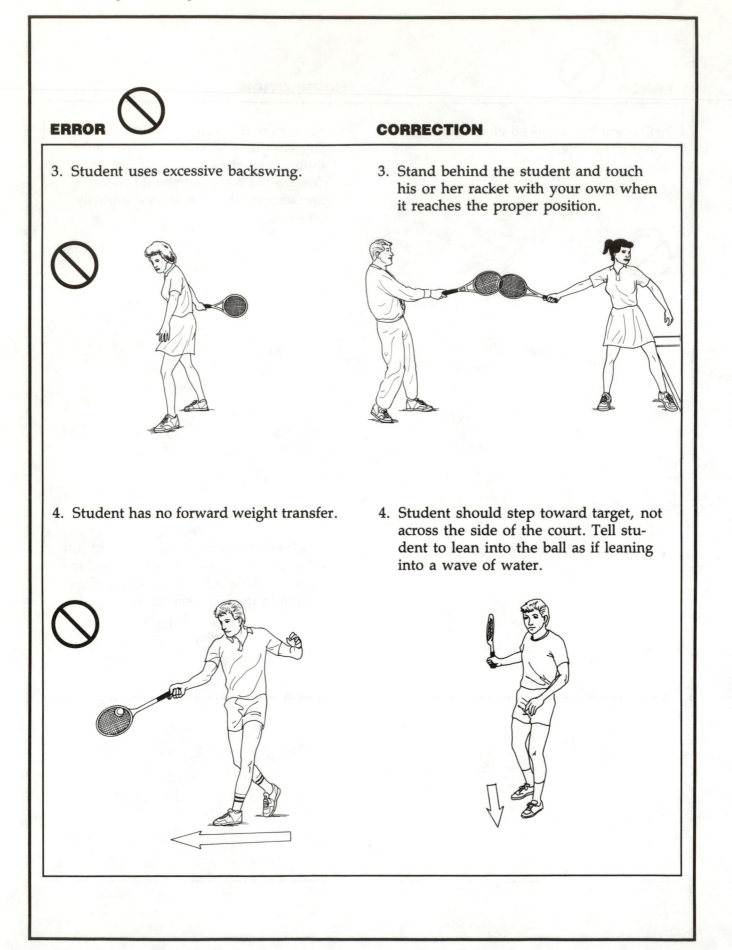

4. Student has no forward weight transfer.

4. Student should step toward target, not across the side of the court. Tell student to lean into the ball as if leaning into a wave of water.

ERROR

CORRECTION

5. Racket swings across front of body.

5. Student should reach out toward the net before the racket crosses the front of the body. Extending the arm rather than swinging with it bent may solve the problem.

BACKHAND

The backhand, the most difficult shot for many players to master, presents problems for most beginning students. There are experts who argue that the backhand is a more natural stroke and should be easier to learn than the forehand. Don't believe it. Instead of hitting on the stronger side, the player has to reach across the front of the body. Students who have played other sports have had practice throwing, reaching, pushing, and hitting, but most of those movements are on the forehand side of the body. Very few sports involve the across-the-body action necessary to hit a backhand. Nevertheless, it is a shot that can be learned and developed into a point-winning stroke.

The beginner has to decide on a one-handed or a two-handed backhand, and changing from the forehand grip while moving and deciding where to hit can be difficult. Getting your students used to the grip will be the big-

gest challenge. You can help your students decide whether to use a one-handed or a two-handed backhand. Generally, students with good forearm strength or a good sense of timing to generate power perform best with a one-handed backhand. Players who are not as strong or who have a natural, smooth-looking two-handed swing can play very effectively with that stroke. Let players experiment both ways before deciding which one to use. If they can hit with either of the two backhand grips, the fundamentals they have learned in the forehand will apply in hitting backhand groundstrokes.

STUDENT KEYS TO SUCCESS

- Turn and move
- Time backswing before ball bounces
- Smooth, even swing
- Make contact early
- Picture a perfect follow-through

Backhand Rating

CHECKPOINT	BEGINNING LEVEL	INTERMEDIATE LEVEL	ADVANCED LEVEL
Preparation	• Runs around the shot • Faces the net • No grip change • Reaches across body	• Smoother footwork • Gets racket back sooner • Uses other hand for support • Changes grips with ease	• Moves into position easily • Weight balanced • Backswing varies according to shot
Swing	• Erratic contact • Racket face too open • Movement at elbow instead of shoulder • Weight on back foot	• Jerky motion • Better direction of ball • Arm extended • Little power or depth • Point of contact more consistent	• Smooth stroke • Solid contact • Can hit offensive shots • Can run and hit with ease • Can use variety of spins
Follow-Through	• None	• Racket continues, but not always in proper direction • Tendency to cross body too soon	• Smooth, flowing • Racket continues out, across, up

Error Detection and Correction for the Backhand

Watch the player's hands first on this stroke. If a one-handed backhand is being used, make sure the opposite hand is on the racket throat to help make the grip change. Players using two hands seldom have grip problems. Be patient. This is a difficult shot to master, and your students will have to learn to work through problems instead of expecting instant success.

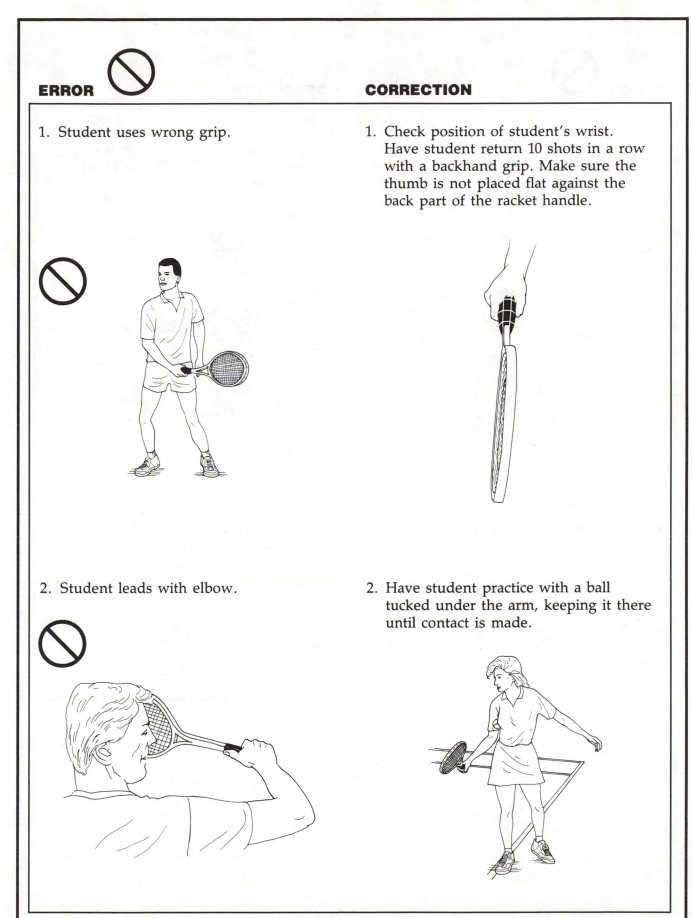

ERROR

1. Student uses wrong grip.

CORRECTION

1. Check position of student's wrist. Have student return 10 shots in a row with a backhand grip. Make sure the thumb is not placed flat against the back part of the racket handle.

2. Student leads with elbow.

2. Have student practice with a ball tucked under the arm, keeping it there until contact is made.

ERROR

CORRECTION

3. Weight is on back foot.

3. Student should lean into shot as if leaning into a wave, pushing the shoulder closer to net forward, the body weight following.

4. Student reaches across body to make contact.

4. Tell student to show back to opponent while preparing to hit. Student should rotate shoulders instead of reaching across the front of body.

ERROR   **CORRECTION**

5. Backswing is too high.

5. Have student swing as if drawing a sword out of a sheath and keep the racket head lower than is the natural tendency. Tell student to think of pulling the racket out of the pocket, not the ear.

6. Student has a droopy wrist.

6. Have student keep the racket head higher than the hand. The shaft of the racket and the forehand should almost form a right angle.

ERROR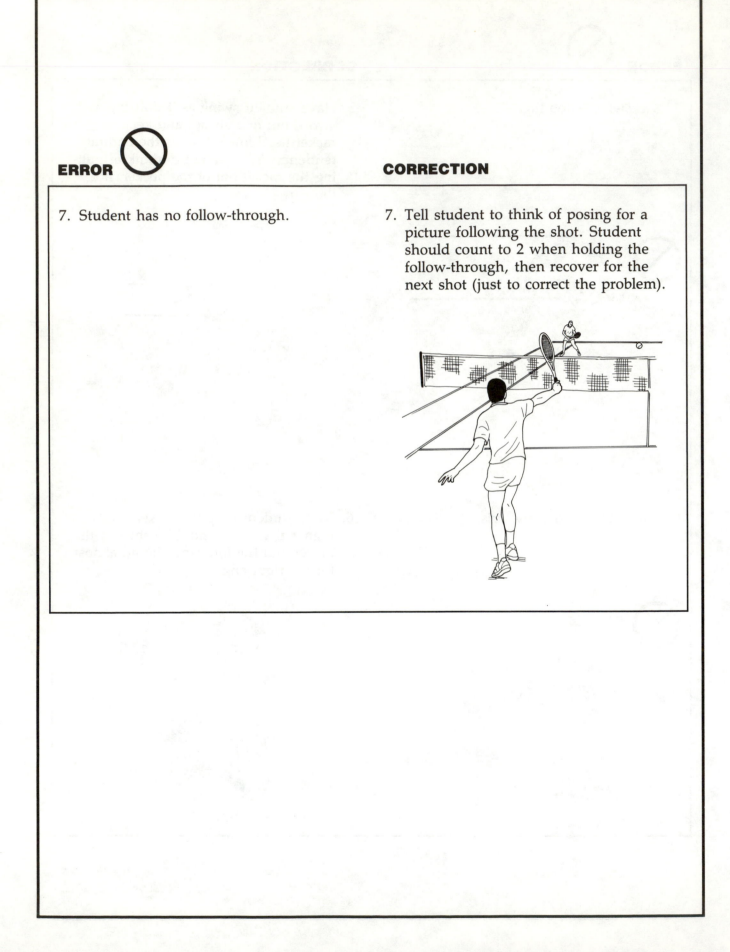

CORRECTION

7. Student has no follow-through.

7. Tell student to think of posing for a picture following the shot. Student should count to 2 when holding the follow-through, then recover for the next shot (just to correct the problem).

Groundstroke Drills

1. *Forehand and Backhand Swings*
[New drill]

Group Management and Safety Tips
- Put up to 16 players on each court.
- Spread students out so they do not hit each other's rackets.
- Work on your own left-handed swing so you can face the group as you lead the students.
- Put left-handers behind you so they can follow you.
- Occasionally have the group freeze on command so you can check body and racket positions.

Equipment
- Rackets, 1 per student

Instructions to Class
- "Find a spot on either the baseline or the service line and face the net. Follow my lead and go through these steps as you swing through the forehand or backhand motion: ready, pivot, step, swing. Concentrate on exactly imitating the swing you see demonstrated in front of you."

Student Option
- "Either watch me and imitate the motion you see, or close your eyes and visualize yourself hitting as you move in response to the commands."

Student Success Goals
- 25 correct forehand swings at the beginning of each lesson
- 25 correct backhand swings at the beginning of each lesson

To Decrease Difficulty
- Have students work in pairs rather than as a group, so they can help each other on a one-to-one basis.
- Let your student swing through selected segments of the swing instead of through the full motion.

To Increase Difficulty
- Increase the number of swings in the Success Goal.
- Create a game in which the object is to maintain a position on the front row: Move a student to the back row if out of position when you give the "freeze" command.

2. Drop and Hit
Forehand Drill
[Corresponds to *Tennis*, Step 3, Drill 2]

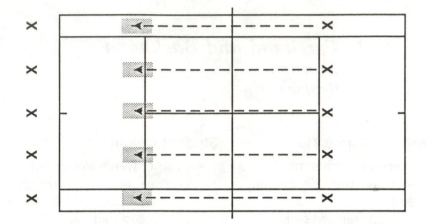

Group Management and Safety Tips

- Place four to ten students on each court, half hitting and half retrieving.
- Retrieve all balls on the opposite side of the hitters or have the retrievers roll the balls back instead of throwing them while players are attempting to hit.

Equipment

- Rackets, 1 per student pair
- Balls, 3 per student pair

Instructions to Class

- "Take a position behind the service line. Extend the arm holding the ball, drop the ball, and hit it across the net with a forehand swing. Let the ball drop; don't bounce it hard against the court. Take your racket back first, then drop and hit. Aim high over the net and deep into the backcourt."

Student Option

- "Count the number of balls hit into the singles backcourt area."

Student Success Goal

- Drop and hit 5 of 10 attempts into the opposite court.

To Decrease Difficulty

- Move student closer to the net.

To Increase Difficulty

- Move player farther from the net.
- Increase the Success Goal by increments of 1.
- Give credit only for shots that land in the singles backcourt.

3. Two-Fingered Forehands or Backhands
[New drill]

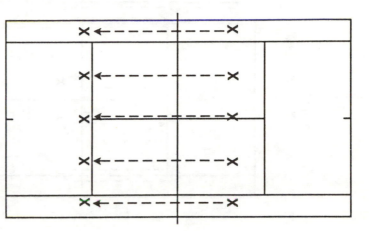

Group Management and Safety Tips

- Use alleys for partners if extra space is needed.
- With 16 players per court, have 4 tossing, 4 hitting, 4 picking up balls, and 4 "shadow swinging" behind the hitters.

Equipment

- Rackets, 1 per student pair
- Balls, 3 per student pair

Instructions to Class

- "Hold the racket in a forehand or backhand grip but use only your thumb and index finger. Hit 20 balls tossed by your partner from a distance of 20 feet. By hitting with only two fingers, you will see how easy these shots can be if the proper grip is used with the thumb and forefinger. Later, using all five fingers will be even easier."

Student Options

- "Increase the distance from the tosser."
- "Alternate using the two-fingered grip with the conventional grip."

Student Success Goals

- 10 of 20 forehand returns using only two-fingered grip
- 10 of 20 backhand returns using only two-fingered grip

To Decrease Difficulty

- Decrease the distance between hitter and tosser.
- Have the tosser toss the ball softly.
- Reduce the Success Goal to 5 of 10.
- Have the partner drop the ball to the hitter's side rather than tossing it to him or her.

To Increase Difficulty

- Increase the distance between hitter and tosser.
- Have the hitter direct shots toward a specific target.
- Increase the Success Goal.

4. Toss to Groundstroke Drill
[Corresponds to *Tennis*, Step 3, Drill 3]

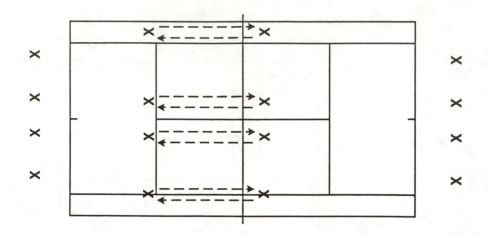

Group Management and Safety Tips

- Use alleys for partners if more space is needed.
- Court can accommodate 16 players, with 4 tossing, 4 hitting, 4 picking up balls, and 4 "shadow swinging" behind the hitters.
- Partners should switch positions after 10 hits.

Equipment

- Rackets, 1 per student pair
- Balls, 3 per student pair

Instructions to Class

- "A tosser stands at the net and sends one-bounce, waist-high tosses to a partner behind the service line. The hitter should aim softly-hit forehands only or backhands only to the tosser. Hitters, try to bump the ball straight back to your partner. Not only does the tosser make a good target, but this also reduces the time you would otherwise have to spend picking up balls."

Student Option

- "Change positions only after hitting 10 shots that your partner can catch with one hand."

Student Success Goals

- 10 of 15 forehand shots hit so that the tosser can catch or reach the ball with one hand
- 10 of 15 backhand shots that the tosser can catch

To Decrease Difficulty

- Allow partners to stand closer to each other.
- Have tosser make softer tosses.
- Reduce Success Goal to 5 of 10 shots.
- Allow the hitter to start with the racket back, pointing to the fence.

To Increase Difficulty

- Increase the distance between partners.
- Increase the Success Goal to 15 of 20.
- Require the tosser to keep one foot planted while trying to catch the ball.

5. Running Forehands or Backhands
[New drill]

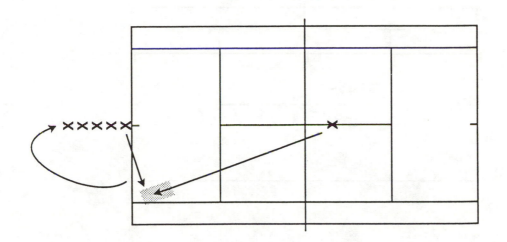

Group Management and Safety Tips

- Have a limit of eight players per court.
- Use students to set up shots with feeds.
- Rotate players between hitting, setting up, and picking up balls.
- Keep the lines moving: one shot, then out of the way.

Equipment

- Rackets, 1 per student
- Balls, 1 basket per court

Instructions to Class

- "Form a line behind the center mark of the baseline. The feeder stands at the net with a basket of balls and tosses or hits a shot to your forehand or backhand. Move, plant your back foot, hit a groundstroke, then return to the end of the line. Try to get to the ball early enough to be on balance when you hit instead of arriving just in time to make contact."

Student Options

- "Work on your own time with a partner setting up shots."
- "Make it a two-shot drill by recovering to the middle of the baseline for a second groundstroke before going to the end of the line."

Student Success Goals

- 10 forehands hit into the singles court
- 10 backhands hit into the singles court

To Decrease Difficulty

- Have feeder set shots up from only a few feet away from the net.
- Have feeder gently toss underhand so that ball bounces waist-high and a racket distance away.
- Have hitter start facing sideline.
- Start hitters at the service line instead of the baseline.

To Increase Difficulty

- Increase the number of consecutive individual or team shots required.
- Have tosser set up shots with more pace.

6. Forehands or Backhands Only

[New drill]

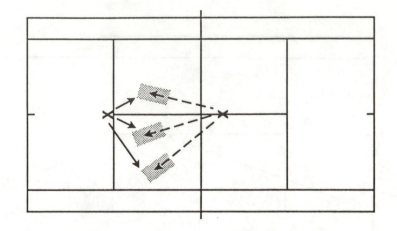

Group Management and Safety Tips

- Put two to four players on each court and use half the court per pair.
- Do not go beyond 45 seconds per round for beginners.
- Use this drill to finish practice sessions or classes.
- Use students not hitting or throwing to pick up balls.
- Remember that this is a footwork and movement drill as much as it is a drill for strokes. Watch the students' feet first, strokes second.

Equipment

- Rackets, 1 per student pair
- Balls, 1 basket per court

Instructions to Class

- "One partner sits at the net with a basket of balls and tosses balls to the other player in the forecourt area for approximately 45 seconds. No matter where the toss is directed, the hitter must maneuver to return the ball with the groundstroke called for. Figure out a way to move your feet and maneuver the racket to hit the ball with the same stroke every time."

Student Options

- "Set personal goals for the number of shots returned during the time allowed."
- "Stay after class to work on your own to improve movement and proportion of returns."

Student Success Goals

- 10 of 15 forehand returns
- 10 of 15 backhand returns

To Decrease Difficulty

- Decrease the length of time per round.
- Have partner toss balls only to the forehand side or directly at the player. This temporarily sacrifices backhand practice so the hitter can gain confidence hitting the easier shot.
- Set a lower Success Goal for the proportion of balls returned.

To Increase Difficulty

- Increase the length of time per round.
- Have partner toss balls to right, center, and left of the service court being used.
- Increase the amount of time per round.
- Increase the Success Goal for the proportion of balls returned.

7. Alleys Only
[New drill]

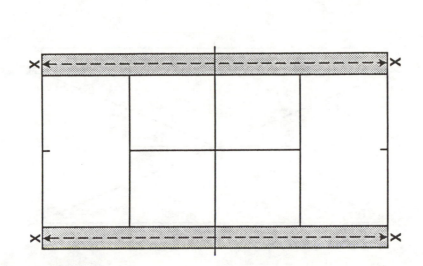

Group Management and Safety Tips

- Encourage soft hitting and good technique.
- If short on court space, use the middle of the court for the same kind of practice, then rotate these students to the alleys.
- At first, match players of equal ability; then get stronger players to take one turn with weaker players.
- Use the drill as part of the class warm-up.

Equipment

- Rackets, 1 per student
- Balls, 3 per student pair

Instructions to Class

- "You and your partner stand on opposite ends of the court, behind the alley. Keep the ball in play with forehands (or backhands, if that is what is being practiced), trying to make all shots land in your partner's alley. Get your feet lined up perfectly, that is, turn your side to the net and step in the direction you want to hit."

Student Options

- "Stand in the alley, halfway between the net and the baseline, or start the drill with both players behind the baseline."
- "Practice forehands only, or backhands only, or alternate the two."

Student Success Goal

- Hit the opposite alley at least 5 times before rotating.

To Decrease Difficulty

- Move players closer to the net.
- Reduce the Success Goal to 2 or 3 hits.
- Allow students to bump the ball softly until they are able to hit stronger shots with control.

To Increase Difficulty

- Require a player to reach the Success Goal before moving up to the baseline.
- Have the student alternate forehand and backhand shots.
- Increase the Success Goal to 7 hits.

8. Consecutive Forehands or Backhands
[New drill]

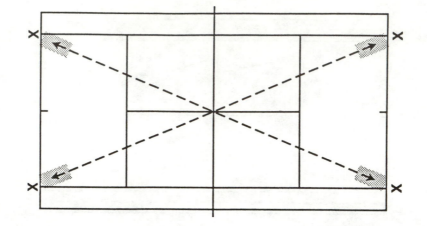

Group Management and Safety Tips

- Put four players on each court at a time; two working on crosscourt forehands in the even court and two others hitting crosscourt backhands in the odd court.
- Do not allow players to run around their backhand crosscourt hits.
- Use nonhitting players to pick up balls.
- Rotate players often enough to prevent inactivity.
- Place beginning and intermediate players behind the service lines.
- Place left-handers opposite each other when possible.

Equipment

- Rackets, 1 per student
- Balls, 3 per student pair

Instructions to Class

- "Stand behind the baseline, toward the corner where you hit with your forehand [or backhand] and diagonally opposite your partner. Put the ball into play and hit consecutive crosscourt groundstrokes. Get to every shot after one bounce. Play balls whether they are inside the boundary lines or not."

Student Option

- "Set individual goals in addition to the Success Goal."

Student Success Goals

- 50 forehand crosscourt shots
- 50 backhand crosscourt shots

To Decrease Difficulty

- Move player closer to the net, where softer groundstrokes can be hit.
- Reduce the Success Goal to 25 attempts.
- Allow a better player to work with a weaker player, to keep the ball in play longer.
- Allow a weaker player to return shots after two bounces.

To Increase Difficulty

- Increase the Success Goal to 75 groundstrokes.
- Require players to rotate out after every error.

9. 2-Minute Drill
[New drill]

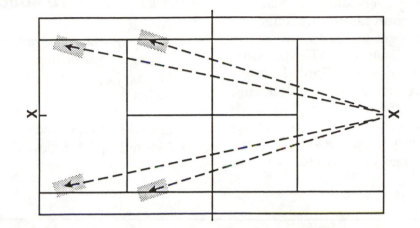

Group Management and Safety Tips

- Keep the feeder supplied with enough balls to hit for 2 minutes.
- Use stronger students as feeders if others cannot set up shots properly.

Equipment

- Rackets, 1 per student
- Balls, 1 basket per court

Instructions to Class

- "A feeder stands at a baseline with a basket of balls and hits shots to a partner on the opposite end. The partner has to get to every shot for 2 minutes. Work hard. Be determined to get to each ball regardless of where it is hit. Concentrate twice as hard during the last part of the drill to compensate for the fatigue you will feel. The feeder keeps firing shots. Don't wait for the return."

Student Options

- "Set personal goals to fit your own ability level."
- "Work on depth as well as returning shots."

Student Success Goal

- 2-minute hitting session

To Decrease Difficulty

- Reduce the Success Goal by 30-second increments.
- Have feeder use softer shots.
- Have feeder send shots only to the forecourt area.

To Increase Difficulty

- Have the feeder increase the depth and side-to-side range of setups.
- Increase the Success Goal by 30-second increments.
- Have partner return all shots with forehands only or backhands only.

Step 4 Groundstroke Combinations

When you watch players stay in a relatively small area of the court and hit forehands or backhands, you begin to get an idea of the ability levels of those players. When the same players have to hit, move all around the court, and change between forehand and backhand strokes, the picture becomes very clear. Even an inexperienced teacher can begin to recognize the skills or lack of skills that indicate beginning, intermediate, and advanced levels of play.

STUDENT KEYS TO SUCCESS

- Anticipate shots
- Move into position quickly
- Change grips without thinking
- Change grips when ball leaves opponent's racket
- Have confidence with both strokes
- Hit with smooth look
- Use full, quick follow-through

Groundstroke Combination Rating

CHECKPOINT	BEGINNING LEVEL	INTERMEDIATE LEVEL	ADVANCED LEVEL
Preparation	• May not change grips • Sluggish footwork • Uneven, jerky backswing • May not use hand for support	• Begins to anticipate shots • Uses the off hand for support • More active with feet • Earlier backswing, but may not be in proper position	• Immediate grip changes • Early shoulder turns • Can anticipate shots • Smooth, flowing movement • Works hard between shots
Swing	• Stabs at the ball • Hits with the wrong grip • Hits off the wrong foot • Moving and hitting coordination poor	• Uses fuller motion • Can time bounce of ball better • Does not avoid backhands • Makes solid contact more often • Can direct shots	• Takes full swings • Looks comfortable hitting • Makes solid contact • Hits with direction and pace • Uses a variety of shots • Can get out of trouble with shots

CHECKPOINT	BEGINNING LEVEL	INTERMEDIATE LEVEL	ADVANCED LEVEL
Follow-Through	• Incomplete • Swing stops with contact	• Full, but racket may be in wrong position (too high or too low)	• Hits through shots • Quick recovery

Error Detection and Correction for Groundstroke Combinations

As players begin to move and hit, it will be more difficult for you to detect errors. Do not look at the big picture, the whole movement and motion of the player. Concentrate on specific areas of the body or on the position of the racket, so you can make very pertinent suggestions to help the student.

ERROR

CORRECTION

ERROR	CORRECTION
1. Student uses wrong grip.	1. There is no quick cure for this. Have the student hit hundreds of balls and constantly check the grip. There must be support with part of the hand behind the racket handle on both the forehand and the backhand.
2. Weight is on back foot.	2. Stand behind the player and give verbal cues to step into the ball. Have player step toward target, not across, and not retreating to hit unless there is no other choice.

ERROR 🚫	CORRECTION
3. Student runs through the shot.	3. Tell student to move, plant, and swing. Recovery for next shot begins during hitting. The student must think about the possibility of having to cover the opposite corner if the opponent returns the shot.
4. Student has a tucked elbow.	4. Tell student to extend the arm as if sweeping dishes off a table. The arm starts tucked but extends as player swings, reaching out to hit.
5. Student exhibits a lack of control.	5. The student must compensate for the body's movement. If student is running forward, swing needs to be reduced. If moving to the side, the ball will drift in that direction. If running back, swing needs to be harder.

Groundstroke Combination Drills

Note: For the remaining drills in this book, assume that all players need rackets.

1. *Running Groundstrokes*
[Corresponds to *Tennis*, Step 4, Drill 1]

Group Management and Safety Tips
- Use feeders with the ability to toss or hit to the right spots.
- Have eight or less hitters in each line.
- Keep the lines moving.
- Rotate players between hitting, setting up, and picking up balls.

Equipment
- Balls, 1 basket per court

Instructions to Class
- "Form a single-file line behind the center mark of the baseline. The feeder stands at the net with a basket of balls and tosses or hits shots alternately to the forehand and backhand. As hitter, move, plant your foot, and hit one forehand; then do the same to hit one backhand and move to the end of the line. You will reach your Success Goal after several turns. Don't watch to see where your first shot goes; immediately start preparing for the next one."

Student Option
- "Work on your own time with a partner setting up shots. With only two players, increase the number of consecutive shots you attempt before switching roles."

Student Success Goal
- 10 consecutive groundstrokes hit into the singles court

To Decrease Difficulty
- Have feeder set up shots a few feet away from the net.
- Start hitter at the service line instead of the baseline; have feeder toss softly.
- Reduce Success Goal to 8 or 6.

To Increase Difficulty
- Have feeder set up shots in a wider area of the court.
- Increase the pace of the setup shots.
- Increase the Success Goal by 5 shots per round.

2. *Consecutive Groundstrokes*
[New drill]

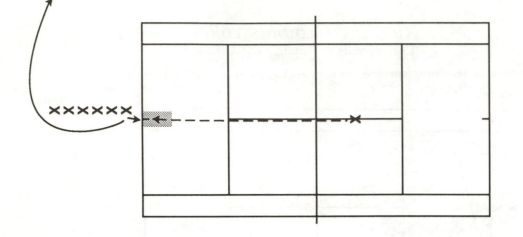

Group Management and Safety Tips

- Keep lines even to avoid waiting.
- Use advanced players as feeders.
- Give weaker players two or three chances to get started.
- Rotate players out occasionally to pick up balls.

Equipment

- Balls, 1 basket per court

Instructions to Class

- ''Form a line behind the baseline. A feeder will stand at the net and put the ball into play to the first hitter in the line. The hitter and feeder keep the ball in play as long as possible, hitting forehand and backhand groundstrokes. The feeder will count the number of total hits in the exchange. When there's a miss, the hitter moves to the back of the line on the next court.''

Student Options

- ''Set personal goals for the number of consecutive shots returned.''
- ''Request more shots to your weaker side.''

Student Success Goal

- Multiples of 5 consecutive groundstrokes, depending on ability level; when goal of 5 is reached, move on to 10, then 15, 20, and so on.

To Decrease Difficulty

- Allow weaker hitter to start from the service line.
- Instruct the hitter and feeder to play all shots, whether in or out.
- Have the feeder set up most shots to the player's stronger side.

To Increase Difficulty

- Have feeder set up shots to a wider area of the court.
- Instruct the feeder to play only shots hit to the singles court.
- Have feeder set up most shots to the hitter's weaker side.
- Set Success Goals in multiples of 10 rather than 5.

3. 4-Point Games
[New drill]

Group Management and Safety Tips

- Begin with more experienced players acting as feeders.
- Place the feeders at the net, service, or baseline, depending on ability (weakest players feed from baseline).
- Introduce the basics of keeping score by using "15, 30, 40, game," as well as no-ad scoring.

Equipment

- Balls, 1 basket per court

Instructions to Class

- "Form a line behind the baseline. The feeder at the net, service line, or baseline on the opposite side will put a ball into play. Play the point out using only groundstrokes. The feeder will attempt to keep the ball in play rather than hit winners. The first player to win 4 points wins the game. If you win, take the feeder's place. If you lose, go to the end of the line on the next court."

Student Option

- "Request that shots be placed to your weaker side."

Student Success Goal

- Individual goal set by instructor according to ability (e.g., for beginners, score at least 1 point in a game; for intermediates, score 2 or 3 points; for advanced players, win at least 1 game).

To Decrease Difficulty

- Allow weaker hitter to start at the service line.
- Instruct feeder to hit most shots to the hitter's stronger side.
- Instruct feeder to play every shot, not just those in the singles court.

To Increase Difficulty

- Have feeder set up shots to a wider area of the court.
- Have feeder increase the pace and depth of setups.
- Have feeder play only shots returned to his or her backcourt area.

4. Crank City
[New drill]

Group Management and Safety Tips

- If using multiple courts, call out the type of shot for all courts at the same time.
- Use only the 50% and 75% speeds for beginners and intermediates; at these levels, players are not ready to hit at 100% velocity with control.
- Allow 1 minute for each round of shots.

Equipment

- Balls, 1 basket per court

Instructions to Class

- "A feeder sets up shots, and a hitter returns from the baseline with groundstrokes. The hitter is in 'Crank City' and has to hit at whatever pace is called for by me or the feeder. Start at 50% velocity, then go to 75%, then to 100%. Later, change the velocity requirement from shot to shot. The important thing is learn to hit at a variety of paces. Do not worry about hitting exactly at 50% or 75% unless you are told to increase or decrease the pace of the ball."

Student Option

- "Work with a partner on your own and direct shots toward target areas as you change pace."

Student Success Goal

- 20 shots at each speed level

To Decrease Difficulty

- Have feeder set up softer shots.
- Have feeder set up shots to a smaller area of the court.
- Have feeder set up shots to the stronger side of the hitter.

To Increase Difficulty

- Have feeder set up shots with more pace to a larger area of the court.
- Have feeder set up shots to the weaker side of the hitter.
- Establish target areas for the hitter.

5. Tag-Team Singles
[New drill]

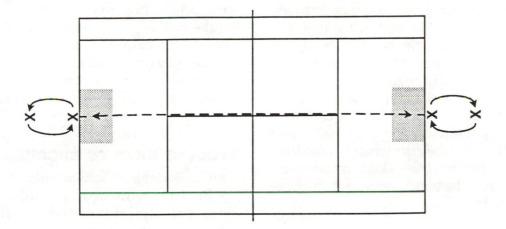

Group Management and Safety Tips

- Balance teams according to ability levels.
- Move between courts to monitor all matches.
- Rotate waiting players in every 3 to 5 minutes.

Equipment

- Balls, 3 per court

Instructions to Class

- "Stand at the baseline, ready to put a ball into play to an opponent on the other baseline. Your partner stands behind you and far enough out of the way not to get hit with your backswing. Drop a ball, put it into play, then get out of the way so your partner can move into position for the return. You and your partner continue alternating shots while your opponents do the same thing. Move after you hit, but always face the net as you move into and out of position."

Student Option

- "Keep score for the number of consecutive 'in' shots either with your partner or to compete against the other team."

Student Success Goal

- Win at least half the games played.

To Decrease Difficulty

- Allow three players on each side to take turns hitting.
- Require all shots to be hit to the forehand side.

To Increase Difficulty

- Allow only the singles court boundaries.
- Rotate players out after three errors.
- Require all players to return with forehands only or backhands only.
- Stipulate that points cannot be earned until the ball has been in play at least 4 times.

Step 5   Beginner's (Punch) Serve

The only players using the punch serve will be beginners you are teaching and others who don't know any other way to serve. Instead of watching players to differentiate between levels of serving ability, just watch to differentiate the beginners who need to spend time practicing at this progression level from those who can immediately progress to a full-swing service motion. Students who can bypass this chapter can be recognized by the ease with which they put the service parts together and by the ball control they demonstrate; students who cannot perform these skills should spend time mastering the punch serve motion before going to Step 6.

Do not worry too much about technique with the punch serve. Within the limits of what you will present in regard to grip, footwork, and swing, give beginners freedom to get the ball in play "their way." The objective is to get them started with a simple serve they can rely on, rather than get into the complicated series of movements necessary for an effective, tournament-level serve. There will be lots of time for that later.

STUDENT KEYS TO SUCCESS

- Comfortable, forehand grip
- Smooth, controlled, forward toss
- Strong, upward, extended swing
- Out, down, across, finish

Beginner's Serve Rating

CHECKPOINT	BEGINNING LEVEL	INTERMEDIATE LEVEL	ADVANCED LEVEL
Preparation	• Incorrect grip (usually Western forehand) • Erratic toss • No feel for back-scratch position of racket	• Not applicable	• Not applicable
Swing	• Leads with elbow • Swings forward instead of upward • Tosses too low • Does not extend arm • No weight transfer		
Follow-Through	• Short, if at all • Swing stops with contact		

Error Detection and Correction for Beginner's Punch Serve

The distance from the baseline to the opponent's service court, as well as the barrier of the net, is intimidating to most beginners. Let them move up as close as is necessary to start getting the ball over the net and into the service court. Then watch for general fundamental skills rather than tennis skills. Can the player toss a ball with control? Is there good hand-eye coordination? Does the player have enough strength to put pace on the ball? If there are problems in these kinds of areas, work toward correcting them before concentrating on more tennis-specific skills.

ERROR

CORRECTION

1. Student uses Western (frying pan) grip.

1. Have student start with an Eastern forehand, the wrist slightly to the right of the top of the handle for right-handers (to the left of top for left-handers). As the player improves, he or she can move to a Continental grip for the serve.

ERROR

CORRECTION

2. Body faces the net.

2. Have student place the feet at a 45-degree angle to the net (body facing the net post). The side should stay toward the net so the server can twist into the shot with the swing.

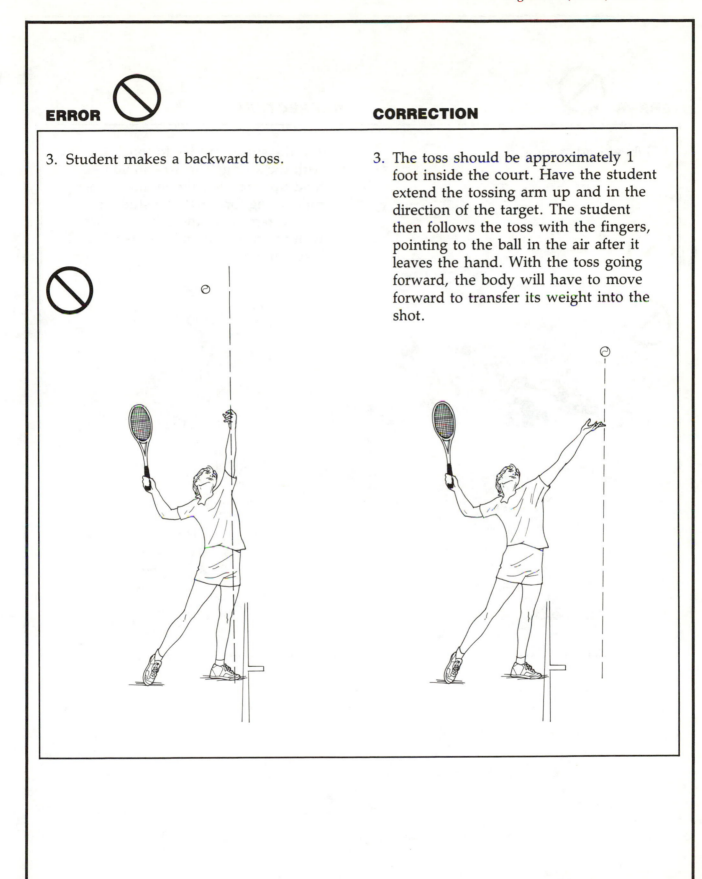

ERROR

CORRECTION

3. Student makes a backward toss.

3. The toss should be approximately 1 foot inside the court. Have the student extend the tossing arm up and in the direction of the target. The student then follows the toss with the fingers, pointing to the ball in the air after it leaves the hand. With the toss going forward, the body will have to move forward to transfer its weight into the shot.

ERROR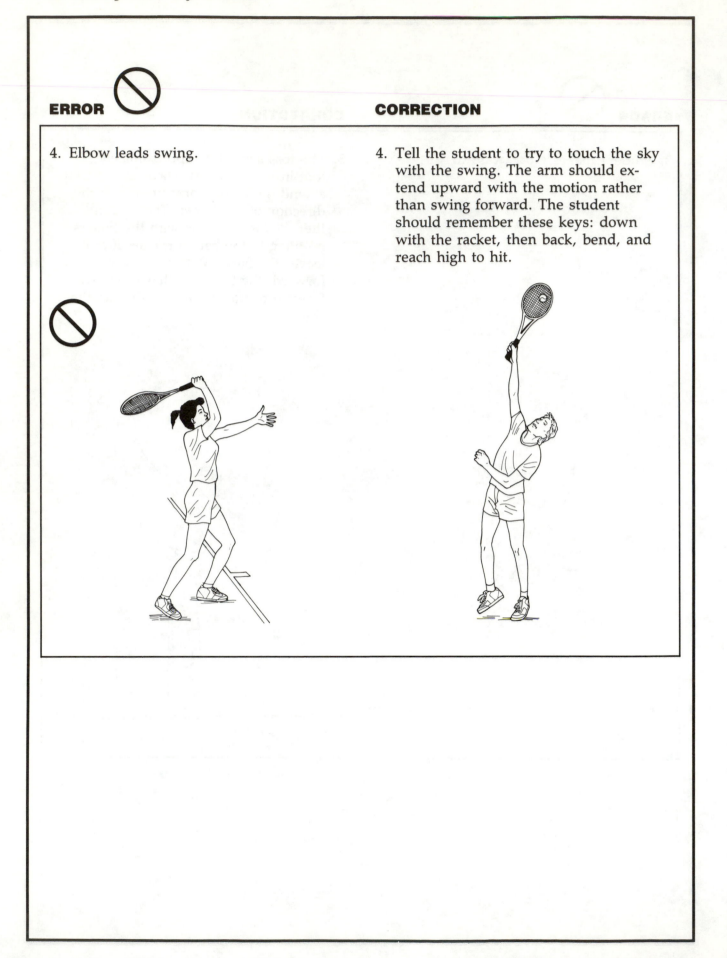

CORRECTION

4. Elbow leads swing.

4. Tell the student to try to touch the sky with the swing. The arm should extend upward with the motion rather than swing forward. The student should remember these keys: down with the racket, then back, bend, and reach high to hit.

ERROR 🚫

CORRECTION

5. Student bends at the waist.

5. The student must not jackknife the body, but should extend fully to make contact. Tell the student to resist the temptation to generate power by pulling the hips back during the swing. Instead, the student should get power with racket speed, timing, and forward movement.

6. Student has difficulty in making contact.

6. Stand next to the server and toss for him or her. Make the server go through the tossing motion to get into the rhythm of the motion, then move away and allow the player to put the swinging and tossing motions together.

1. Punch Serve Throw
[Corresponds to *Tennis*, Step 5, Drill 1]

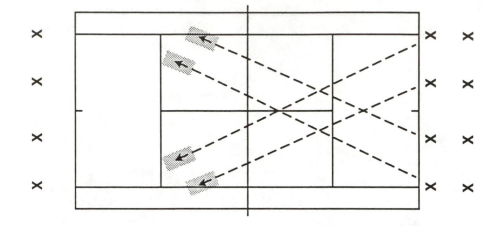

Group Management and Safety Tips

- Place weaker players on a separate court and allow them to toss from the service line instead of the baseline.
- Place eight players on each court.
- Split the class into two groups: one group tosses into the service courts; the other retrieves, then tosses back to the first group, using the correct motion.

Equipment

- Balls, at least 1 basket per court

Instructions to Class

- "Stand behind the baseline. Start by holding a ball behind your head, with your elbow bent. Throw balls into the service court diagonally from where you are standing. Toss with a full, high motion, and release the ball at the top of the motion."
- "Make sure that your weight rocks from back to front."

Student Options

- "On your own, practice throwing to specific targets within the service court."
- "Practice playing catch with a partner at a distance of 30 feet."

Student Success Goal

- 20 consecutive tosses into the proper service court

To Decrease Difficulty

- Move tosser closer to the net.
- Allow tosses anywhere over the net instead of only into a particular service court.

To Increase Difficulty

- Move tosser farther from net.
- Require a full-swing throwing motion.
- Increase the Success Goal by increments of 10.

2. Service Toss Target
[Corresponds to *Tennis*, Step 5, Drill 3]

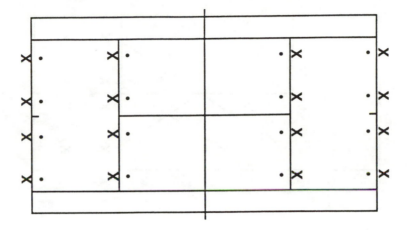

Group Management and Safety Tips

- You can have up to 40 players per court. Spread the players out to give them room to work.
- Have alternate targets available for students with no racket covers.
- Watch for tossing technique as well as target-hitting accuracy.

Equipment

- Ball, 1 per student
- Racket cover or other target, 1 per student

Instructions to Class

- "Find a position on the baseline or the service line and place your racket cover or other object just inside the line. Now practice your toss, letting it drop and hit the target you have placed on the ground. Watch the flight of the ball as it rises in the air and drops to the target. Be sure to extend your arm and fingers upward with the toss."

Student Options

- "Set individual goals."
- "Compete with a partner."
- "Practice on your own to refine the toss."

Student Success Goal

- 5 out of 10 tosses hitting the target

To Decrease Difficulty

- Let the student toss lower. The drill's purpose is to practice controlling the direction of the toss; the exact height of the toss can be adjusted later.
- Reduce the Success Goal to 3 of 10 attempts.

To Increase Difficulty

- Increase the Success Goal to 7 of 10 attempts.
- Have the student practice the toss with a full-swing motion.

3. Service Line Serve

[Corresponds to *Tennis*, Step 5, Drill 5]

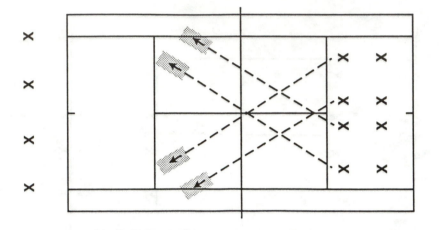

Group Management and Safety Tips

- Divide the class into groups of servers and retrievers. Have the groups switch roles when all the balls have been served to the opposite side.
- Put up to eight servers on each court at one time.
- Stand at the side of the court, even with the service line, in order to observe several servers at a time.

Equipment

- Balls, 1 basket per court

Instructions to Class

- "Take a position at the service line and practice the punch serve into the proper service court. Serve two balls, then move out of the way for the next server. Take your time and get set before the serve. Be deliberate. Variables such as the position of your feet and a correct grip can be taken care of before the serve so you can then concentrate on just hitting the ball. Alternate serving from the left and the right sides."

Student Option

- "If it will not interfere with the others, gradually move back toward the baseline as you master your serve."

Student Success Goal

- 7 out of 10 punch serves to each service court

To Decrease Difficulty

- Reduce the Success Goal to 5 of 10.
- Let the student move inside the service line to serve.

To Increase Difficulty

- Increase the Success Goal to 10 of 10.
- Increase the distance between the servers and the net.

4. *Baseline Serve*

[Corresponds to *Tennis*, Step 5, Drill 6]

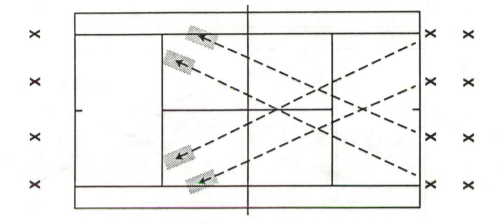

Group Management and Safety Tips

- Place a basket of extra balls against the fence while students are serving.
- Four to six players can serve from a baseline at a time, with the same number waiting behind them.
- Divide the class into groups of servers and retrievers. After a basket of balls has been served, they switch roles.

Equipment

- Balls, 1 basket per court

Instructions to Class

- "Take a position on the baseline and use the correct motion to serve into the proper court. Serve two balls, then move back to allow room for the next server. Alternate serving from the right and left sides. If you must make mistakes, make mistakes deep; it is easier to correct serves that land beyond the service line than it is to solve problems of repeatedly hitting into the net."

Student Options

- "Set individual goals."
- "Compete with a partner for the most balls served into the proper court."

Student Success Goal

- 5 out of 10 serves into each service court

To Decrease Difficulty

- Reduce the Success Goal to 3 of 10.
- Have student move closer to the net for serves.

To Increase Difficulty

- Increase the Success Goal to 7 to 10.
- Have server change from a forehand to a Continental grip.

5. *Long Distance Serve*
[Corresponds to *Tennis*, Step 5, Drill 7]

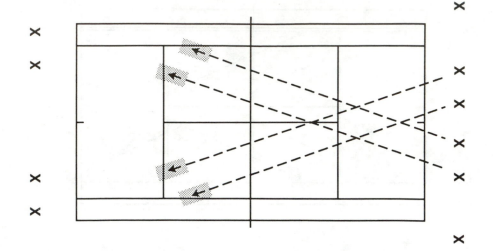

Group Management and Safety Tips

- Divide your class into groups of servers and retrievers that will alternate tasks.
- Place players waiting to serve and tennis balls well out of the way of those serving.
- Four servers stand in position to serve at one time.

Equipment

- Balls, 1 basket per court

Instructions to Class

- ''Take a position 10 feet behind the baseline. Practice serving into the proper court. Serve two balls and move back to allow room for the next server. Serving at a longer distance from the service court should build strength and add to your confidence for when you serve from the normal distance.''

Student Options

- ''Set individual goals.''
- ''Compete with a partner for the most shots hit into the proper court.''

Student Success Goal

- 3 of 10 serves to each service court

To Decrease Difficulty

- Move server closer to the baseline.
- Reduce the Success Goal to 1 or 2 out of 10.

To Increase Difficulty

- Increase the Success Goal to 5 out of 10.
- Have better players change the grip from a forehand to a Continental.

6. *Punch Serve Targets*
[Corresponds to *Tennis*, Step 5, Drill 8]

Group Management and Safety Tips

- Use targets large enough to ensure success by most students.
- Place four to six servers on each court.
- Divide groups into servers and retrievers; then alternate tasks.

Equipment

- Balls, 1 basket per court
- Large cardboard boxes or other targets, 2 per service court (more than two large targets clutter the court)

Instructions to Class

- "Take a position at the baseline and serve, trying to hit the targets placed in the opposite service courts. Serve two balls, then move back to get two more balls while another player takes your place. Get everything set before beginning your service motion. Just before you begin the serve, look out at the target to get a perspective on its distance and location."

Student Options

- "Set individual goals."
- "Compete with a partner for the most targets hit."

Student Success Goal

- 2 of 10 serves hitting targets

To Decrease Difficulty

- Move server closer to the service line.
- Use larger targets.

To Increase Difficulty

- Place targets in specific areas of the service court (the backhand corner, for example).
- Have teams compete for the most targets hit in 20 to 30 serves.
- Increase the Success Goal to 4 of 10.

7. *Serve Return Game*
[Corresponds to *Tennis*, Step 5, Drill 9]

Group Management and Safety Tips

- Place four players on each court, two pairs serving and returning crosscourt.
- Alert students to watch for balls hit by other players.
- Use waiting students to keep score and retrieve balls.
- Require students to hit crosscourt returns only.

Equipment

- Balls, 3 per student pair

Instructions to Class

- ''Play a game with a partner, using only the serve and the service return. Every serve into the proper court counts 1 point; every good return counts 1 point. Do not play the point out; just focus on getting your serves in and your service returns back into the singles court. The first player to score 10 points wins; then switch roles.''

Student Option

- ''Direct serves and returns to mentally targeted areas of the court.''

Student Success Goal

- Win at least half the games played.

To Decrease Difficulty

- Match the player with a lesser opponent.
- Count 2 points for in serves.

To Increase Difficulty

- Match player with a better opponent.
- Subtract points for missed serves or returns.

Step 6 Full-Swing Serve

Players at every level usually at least attempt a full-swing serve. The variety of styles is as diverse as the people who play tennis. So, while there are some fundamental guidelines to be followed, you have to allow for some diversity. There are three reasons not to change a stroke, whether it is a serve, a groundstroke, or any other stroke: Don't suggest a change if (a) the stroke works, (b) the student can develop and improve it, and (c) the player is satisfied with it. Not every tennis player hopes to become a world-class player. If there are students who are content to hit a soft punch serve to get the ball into play and enjoy themselves, let them do it. However, they have to understand that you may award a grade consistent with their limited aspirations.

Teach the full-swing serve as if it had component parts. When these parts are put together, a smooth, continuous motion develops. An important idea is for the player to eliminate as much inconsistency as possible when serving. If the player stands at exactly the same place to serve each time, this is one serve variable that needs no further thought. If the toss goes to the right spot every time, this is another variable that won't go wrong.

If you or your students know how all of these parts are supposed to fit together, faults can be corrected easily. Don't let a student add to a problem by doing things differently on every serve. When a player can correct his or her own faults, you know you are doing a good job of teaching.

STUDENT KEYS TO SUCCESS

- Move hands down and up together
- Use smooth, rhythmic motion
- Move through the shot
- Reach high to hit
- Finish out, across, down

Full-Swing Serve Rating

CHECKPOINT	BEGINNING LEVEL	INTERMEDIATE LEVEL	ADVANCED LEVEL
Preparation	• Holds an Eastern or Western forehand grip • Stands facing the net • Low or inconsistent toss	• Holds a forehand grip • Starts with body at an angle to the net • Has a more consistent toss	• Holds a Continental or backhand grip • Starts with feet more apart • Tosses higher than can reach
Swing	• No backscratch and bent elbow motion • Mis-hits balls • Little pace or spin	• Bends arm, then reaches to hit • Makes solid contact • Inconsistent power serve	• Fluid, upward motion • Extends to hit ball • Uses variety of spins • Seldom double faults

Full-Swing Serve Rating

CHECKPOINT	BEGINNING LEVEL	INTERMEDIATE LEVEL	ADVANCED LEVEL
Follow-Through	• Swing stops with contact	• More complete • Racket finishes down and across	• Body finishes inside the court • Racket finishes with out, across, and down motion

Error Detection and Correction for the Full-Swing Serve

Every player's serving motion looks a little different from those of other players. Do not try to produce serving clones out of your students. Let their bodies figure out ways to produce effective serves, staying within the limits of the fundamentals they have been taught. The objective is to have a serve that works, that is comfortable, and that the player can improve with practice and competition. If a serve meets these criteria, technique will eventually take care of itself.

ERROR 🚫   **CORRECTION**

ERROR	CORRECTION
1. Server has a jerky, segmented swing.	1. Have your student work on smooth, flowing, continuous motion. The hands should go down together, then up together. Have the student slow down the backswing. The idea is to start the motion slowly and deliberately, then to build momentum and speed with the racket head during the swing.
2. Server uses an incorrect grip.	2. As a player's serve improves, he or she should practice using a Continental grip. If allowed to hold an Eastern forehand or, even worse, a Western grip, it will be very difficult to improve.

ERROR **CORRECTION**

3. Server does not move through the shot.

3. If the player finishes the serve with both feet behind the baseline, there is very little power on the serve. Have server toss far enough in front of body to force forward movement. The body should move toward the net during the serving motion.

4. Eyes drop.

4. Have your student keep the head up, and try to see service contact. Use a baseball cap to reinforce this upward focus. Tell your student not to be so anxious to see where the ball is going.

5. Server bends at the waist.

5. Student should not jackknife at the waist but should extend like a straight arrow to hit. The player should shoot up into the air to make contact, instead of letting the ball drop down to eye level.

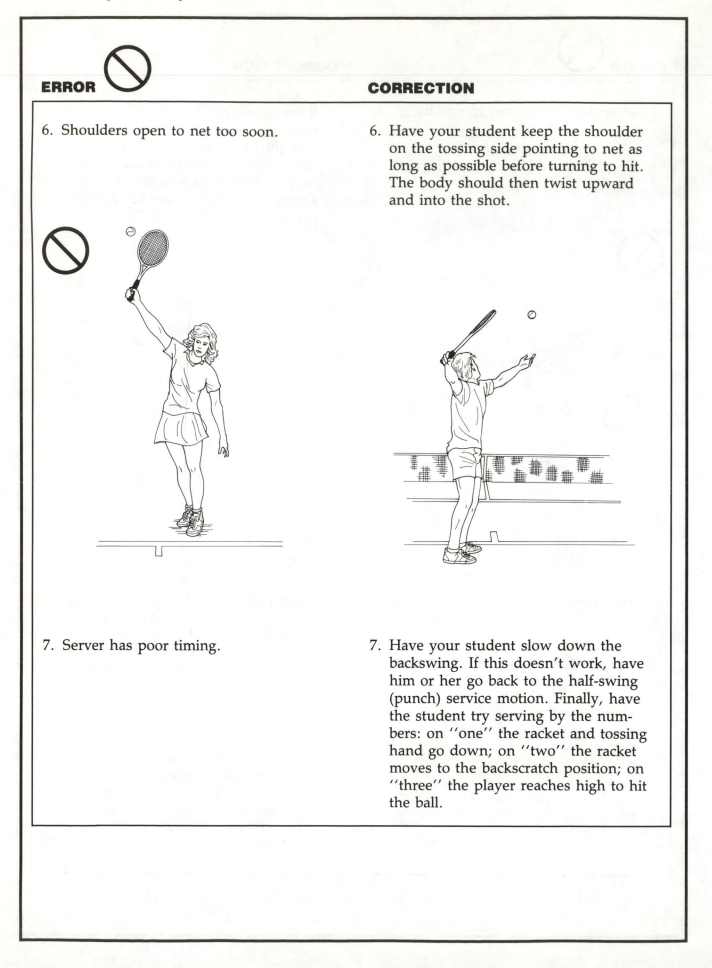

ERROR

CORRECTION

6. Shoulders open to net too soon.

6. Have your student keep the shoulder on the tossing side pointing to net as long as possible before turning to hit. The body should then twist upward and into the shot.

7. Server has poor timing.

7. Have your student slow down the backswing. If this doesn't work, have him or her go back to the half-swing (punch) service motion. Finally, have the student try serving by the numbers: on "one" the racket and tossing hand go down; on "two" the racket moves to the backscratch position; on "three" the player reaches high to hit the ball.

Full-Swing Serve Drills

1. *Racket Cover Serves*
[Corresponds to *Tennis*, Step 6, Drill 1]

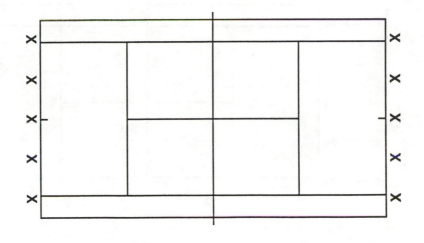

Group Management and Safety Tips

- Put up to 40 players on each court, using both sides of the court.
- Space students far enough apart to avoid accidental racket contact.

Equipment

- Rackets with racket covers, 1 per student

Instructions to Class

- "Find a position along the service line or the baseline. Practice the service motion with the racket cover on your racket. The added resistance to the air should make you stronger and make serving without resistance easier. Keep your eyes up and try to imagine yourself hitting a ball."

Student Option

- "Place a lightweight object inside the cover for more resistance."

Student Success Goal

- 25 full-swing service motions

To Decrease Difficulty

- Reduce the Success Goal to 20, 15, or 10 swings.
- Have your student take the racket cover off to swing through the serving motion.

To Increase Difficulty

- Increase the Success Goal by increments of 5.
- Increase the amount of weight inside the racket cover.

2. *Fence Serves*
[Corresponds to *Tennis*, Step 6, Drill 3]

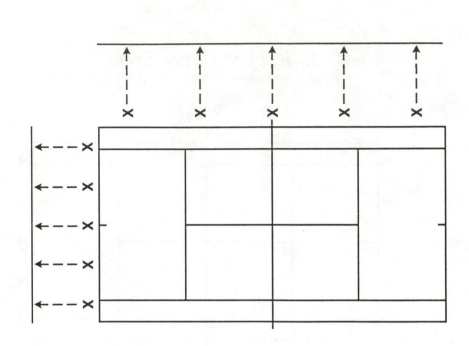

Group Management and Safety Tips

- Put 10 to 15 players on each court.
- Position students far enough from each other to avoid their getting hit by stray shots.
- Give "serve" and "pick up" commands to avoid accidents.
- Move weaker students closer to the wall or fence. All students should be serving straight ahead, and with enough space not to be in danger of getting hit by other servers.

Equipment

- Balls, 3 per student
- Fence or wall surrounding the courts, with space for every student

Instructions to Class

- "Find a position approximately 15 feet from a wall or a fence. Practice serving into the fence. Work on rhythm and timing more than on aiming for targets on the fence, but direct your serves at a height of about 8 feet."

Student Option

- "Direct your serves at a target on the fence. Still, work on technique more than accuracy."

Student Success Goal

- 25 serves

To Decrease Difficulty

- Move student closer to the fence.

To Increase Difficulty

- Increase the Success Goal by increments of 5.
- Have your student aim for a specific point on the fence (at least 8 feet high).

3. Segmented Serves
[New drill]

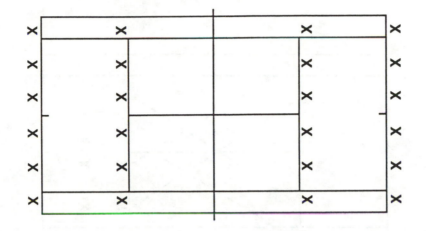

Group Management and Safety Tips

- Put up to 40 players on each court.
- Stop the group or an individual to make a point.
- Face the group and swing with them, if possible.
- Space the students to avoid accidental racket contact.

Equipment

- Rackets, 1 per student

Instructions to Class

- "Find a position on the service line or the baseline. Follow my lead as we practice these parts of the service motion: (1) down with the arm and the racket; (2) down, back, bend; and (3) down, back, bend, reach high with the racket."

Student Option

- "Simulate the toss with the opposite arm as you go through the rhythmic motion with the serving arm."

Student Success Goal

- 25 full-swing service motions

To Decrease Difficulty

- Allow students to work in pairs rather than with entire group. The one-on-one practice can be like looking into the mirror to serve. If one player is off in the motion, the other may be able to help.

To Increase Difficulty

- Increase the Success Goal by increments of 5.
- Have student close eyes and visualize the swing.

4. *Service Line Serves*
[New drill]

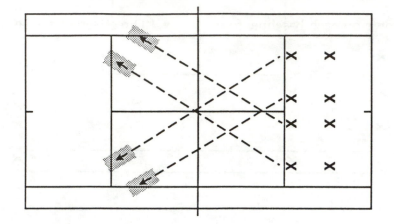

Group Management and Safety Tips

- Put four students on the service line at a time.
- Rotate four more players in to serve; use four more to retrieve balls.
- Require waiting players to stand at least 15 feet behind the servers.
- Place the basket of balls at least 15 feet behind the servers.

Equipment

- Balls, 1 basket per court

Instructions to Class

- ''Take a position at the service line. Practice serves using the full-swing motion. Serve two balls, then move back to make room for the next server. Get set first; take your time; keep your head up as you reach to hit. Try to block everything un-necessary from your mind. The serve is one shot in tennis in which you have complete control. The opposing players or others around the court should not even be considered; they are just distractions. Your serve is all up to you.''

Student Options

- ''Direct your serves to target areas.''
- ''Compete with partners for the most in serves.''

Student Success Goal

- 10 of 20 serves into opposite service court

To Decrease Difficulty

- Move the server closer to the net.

To Increase Difficulty

- Gradually move the server nearer the baseline.

5. Baseline Serves
[New drill]

Group Management and Safety Tips

- Put four students on each baseline, four ready to rotate in to serve, and four more retrieving balls on the opposite baseline.
- Require waiting players to stand at least 15 feet behind the servers.
- Place the basket of balls at least 15 feet behind the servers.
- Rotate players every 3 minutes.

Equipment

- Balls, 1 basket per court

Instructions to Class

- "Take a position at the baseline. Practice serves using the full-swing motion. Serve two balls, then move back to make room for the next server. Get set before you serve. Do not 'walk through' the motion. Be deliberate without taking too much time."

Student Options

- "Direct serves to the backhand or forehand target areas."
- "Compete with partners for the most in serves."

Student Success Goal

- 5 of 20 serves into the opposite service court

To Decrease Difficulty

- Move the server one step inside the baseline.
- Allow the server to use the half-swing motion for two or three serves to regain timing and accuracy, if necessary.

To Increase Difficulty

- Place racket covers, tennis ball cans, or stacked tennis balls in the service courts as targets.

6. *Team Serving Contest*
[New drill]

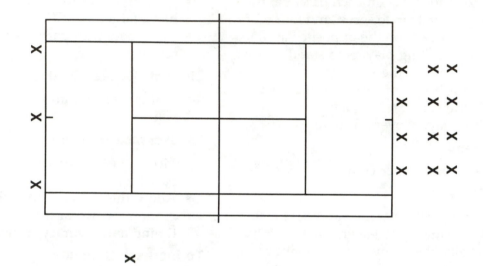

Group Management and Safety Tips

- Put up to 12 players on each court.
- Position scorekeepers to the sides of the service courts.
- Balance teams with combinations of strong and weak servers.

Equipment

- Balls, at least 1 basket per court

Instructions to Class

- "All the players on your court will compete against the players on the other courts for the most serves in. Four players may serve at the same time. Serve two balls, then move back and out of the way to get two more balls. Two classmates will keep score by counting the number of serves hit into the proper court."

Student Option

- "Use the punch serve if you are not ready for full swings."

Student Success Goal

- Participate in at least one team-serving contest

To Decrease Difficulty

- Allow a weaker server to use the punch (half-swing) serve.

To Increase Difficulty

- Allow stronger servers only one attempt and weaker servers two attempts.

7. Long-Distance Serves
[New drill]

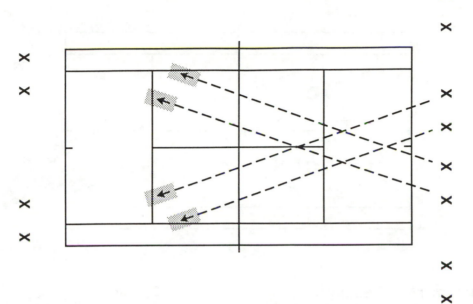

Group Management and Safety Tips

- Have four players per court serve at a time.
- Waiting players should stand to the side and out of the way.

Equipment

- Balls, 1 basket per court

Instructions to Class

- "Find a position behind the baseline and near the fence to practice serves. Don't change your motion; just hit higher and deeper than normal. Serving from a long distance should make serving from the baseline easier."

Student Option

- "Count the number of consecutive serves in from the long-distance position."

Student Success Goal

- 10 of 20 serves into the opposite service court

To Decrease Difficulty

- Move server closer to the baseline.

To Increase Difficulty

- Increase the Success Goal by increments of 2.

8. Target Serves
[Corresponds to *Tennis*, Step 6, Drill 5]

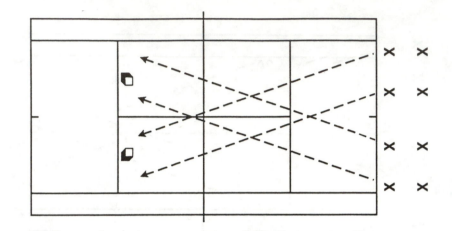

Group Management and Safety Tips

- Put four to six players on each court.
- Use targets large enough to ensure success.
- Stop the drill when a target is hit, to move it back into place.

Equipment

- Balls, 1 basket per court
- Large boxes or other targets

Instructions to Class

- "Take a position on the baseline. Serve and try to hit the target placed in the service court area. Serve two balls, then move back to allow the next player to serve. Look to get a perspective on target distance and location before you start the motion. Before the toss, try to imagine yourself swinging at the ball and placing it where you want to go. The placement of the targets is just to give you something on which to focus. Serving to take advantage of the receiver's weaknesses will come later, when you will aim at mental targets in the backhand corners or in positions left open by the receiver."

Student Options

- "Try to concentrate on technique, even if it costs in accuracy."
- "Move the targets to various areas of the service court."

Student Success Goal

- 3 of 10 serves hitting targets

To Decrease Difficulty

- Move the player closer to the net.
- Use larger targets.
- Reduce the Success Goal to 1 or 2 out of 10.

To Increase Difficulty

- Use smaller targets.
- Increase the Success Goal by increments of 1.

9. Serve and Return Games
[Corresponds to *Tennis*, Step 6, Drill 6]

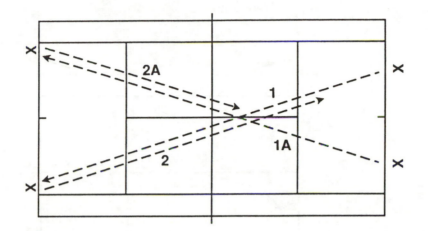

Group Management and Safety Tips

- Two games may be played simultaneously on the same court.
- Put four players on each court, two serving and two returning crosscourt.
- Use a handicap system if two players of unequal ability play each other.

Equipment

- Balls, at least 3 balls per student pair

Instructions to Class

- "Play with a partner, using only the serve and the service return. Every serve into the proper court counts 1 point, and every return counts 1 point. The server gets two chances to get the ball in play. The first partner to score 10 points wins. If you are serving, do not worry about whether your opponent will get the shot back. Your job is to get the ball into play with a serve; let the other player worry about getting it back."

Student Option

- "Alternate serves and returns after every game. Take turns being the server and receiver after every 10-point game."

Student Success Goal

- Play at least 6 games.

To Decrease Difficulty

- Award the player 2 points for serves and returns when paired against a better opponent.

To Increase Difficulty

- Require the stronger player to stand closer to receive and farther to serve.

10. One-Serve Games
[New drill]

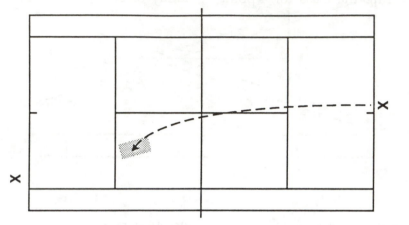

Group Management and Safety Tips

- Put two players on each court.
- Rotate waiting players in as often as possible.
- If players are unequal in ability, enforce the one-serve rule only for the stronger player.

Equipment

- Balls, 3 per student pair

Instructions to Class

- ''Play a game against a classmate in which you get only one serve to put the ball into play.''

Student Option

- ''Use no-ad or conventional scoring.''

Student Success Goal

- Get every serve in for at least one game.

To Decrease Difficulty

- Allow the player to serve as if hitting a second serve.

To Increase Difficulty

- Require player to attempt normally paced first serves.

Step 7 Three-Shot Singles

At this point, your students should be able to begin playing simple games using the punch serve, the forehand, and the backhand. Schedule time during the class for 4-point games (first player to win 4 points), alternating pairs of opponents as quickly as possible. Encourage everyone to find time on their own to play games with friends and classmates, using conventional scoring.

Watch for movement problems and for stroke flaws that develop because of your students' trying to hit and move at the same time. Your students will begin to have a better feel for what the game is like, and they will recognize the need for doing more drill work. If you haven't divided the class into ability groups by now, this type of competition will make your task easy. You will probably discover that some players who did well in drills do not do as well in game situations, whereas others who looked bad practicing perform very well in competition.

Following are things to look for as you evaluate basic playing skills. If problems are noted, use the drills in this book to improve technique, concentration, and strategy. The purpose of this step is to allow players to start playing actual games. Do not interrupt play frequently with talk and tips.

WINS AND LOSSES

Watch for players who enjoy winning, who can win and lose gracefully, and whose level of skill moves up with competition instead of decreasing. For some, this will be the first time they have competed in tennis; for others, this will be the first time they have competed in *any* sport. In either case, it is important for such players to keep tennis in perspective. If there are problems, talk to these students privately and explain what their objectives should be during this part of the course. There are plenty of opportunities for serious, competitive tennis outside of the class environment. During class competition, players should certainly be intense, and they should want to win, but not at the expense of alienating themselves from other classmates or getting into trouble with you.

STROKE TECHNIQUE

The players who practice the techniques learned in class, even if it costs them points and games now, will be better players in the long run. At the beginning level, it is easier to win with poor technique than with proper form. This quick thrill of victory will be paid for when the player with poor technique realizes that it prevents further stroke development. Watch for players whose practice skills break down in match play. Work to get them to keep trying to hit and move correctly regardless of the score in a set or match. Encourage students who might be losing while using the skills taught and learned in class; these good strokes will pay off in the long run.

CONCENTRATION

Notice players' eyes during and between points. Players who can completely focus on the task at hand and who can keep their eyes off the bleachers and other courtside distractions have a tremendous advantage over other less intense players. Help players keep their attention focused on the ball and the match they are playing. Constantly remind them to think about what they are supposed to be doing rather than to let their minds drift to distractions. Try placing them on courts where there is the least amount of outside interference. Have them read Step 18 in *Tennis: Steps to Success* for more specific tips on improving concentration.

EMOTIONAL CONTROL

Do not permit yelling, screaming, pouting, racket throwing, cursing, or other kinds of undesirable behavior seen, and frequently tolerated, in tennis. Emotional control is learned just as other skills are learned. Start helping your students develop such control the first day they walk onto the court. You will not only help them avoid public embarrassment, but you will also help them be better players by channeling strong emotions into productive, game-winning energy.

Establish rules for unacceptable behavior. Point-penalty systems (the loss of points or games during competition due to bad behavior) work as effectively in class as they do in matches. Explain at the beginning of the course that students may be asked to sit out during class competition if their behavior is unsportsmanlike; this may also help students keep their emotions under control.

MOVEMENT SKILLS

Watch your players' feet. Look for action, early preparation, and balance. Getting to the ball just in time to make a shot is not as good as getting there early, setting up properly, and hitting from a comfortable, solid position. Your standing behind a court and telling a player to recover after hitting a shot works for many students. ''Hit and move'' is a phrase that reminds players not to hit, then stand and admire shots. Drills that force players to cover open parts of the court also help. The ''Footwork Drill'' (Step 2, Drill 6), ''Forehands or Backhands Only'' (Step 3, Drill 6), and the ''2-Minute Drill'' (Step 3, Drill 9) are other examples of exercises that improve court movement.

AGGRESSIVENESS

Try to instill the idea of having a ''killer instinct'' in points and games. This does not have anything to do with personality, but rather the ability to put the ball away at the right time during a point and to close out a set or a match instead of letting an opponent get back into the match. Some players are too nice for their own good. Work with players to increase concentration on important (game-deciding) points.

Be careful that aggressiveness is tempered with patience, though. Many young players want to get the point over with even when they are not in a position to do so. Encourage them to constantly improve their position during points until it is time to put shots away. At the intermediate level, shot selection (knowing when to hit certain shots) is a very difficult concept to master. Putting players in game situations and observing how they select shots is your responsibility as instructor. Taking your advice is the sign of a maturing tennis player.

PATIENCE

The better player usually wins in tennis; the longer two players are on the court during a match, the more likely it is that the better player will win. Thus, patience is very important. Most points in tennis are lost by poor shots rather than won with winners. Teach your students not to get too discouraged if they have a series of bad points or even games and not to get too high when things are going extremely well. The consistent, patient player who is fundamentally sound can beat the player whose mood swings and whose level of play changes dramatically during a match. Teach students to (a) get into the point with relatively safe shots, (b) work into a position of being able to control the point, and (c) finish the point when an opening exists or a weakness is evident. Too many inexperienced players start out trying to win the point on the first or second shot, just hang on if that doesn't work, then get too conservative if things go bad.

WILLINGNESS TO TRY NEW SHOTS

One of the things that makes tennis fun is the challenge of hitting creative and even difficult shots. Although good judgment has to be used when attempting such shots, players with a flair and an interest in going beyond routine strokes demonstrate a healthy curiosity that will benefit them later. Teach your players to try creative shots when they are comfortably ahead in games and sets—but not when the match is on the line. Taking time in practice to try such shots as topspin forehands, twist serves, and offensive lobs will make players more comfortable trying the same shots during competition. Also, playing the same point and situation several times will give players confidence to try new shots during matches.

ABILITY TO GET OUT OF TROUBLE

A good shot will win the point against an average player. A good player will get to that same shot and get it back. A great player will get to the shot and hit it back for a winner.

Try to get your students into a frame of mind in which they think they have a chance not only to get everything back but even to win some points when they are in trouble. Set goals of getting at least one ''impossible'' return back in every game. Take time in practice for the ''Take-Your-Best-Shot-Drill'' (Step 18, Drill 4). Give one player any easy setup he or she loves to hit, then play the point out. See how many times out of 10 points the underdog can return the ''best shot'' and win the point.

ENJOYMENT OF THE GAME

Remind your class that tennis is only a game. The purpose is to have fun and get exercise while doing it. You may have to work on a slight attitude adjustment for students who treat this game as if it were a life-and-death battle. Controlled intensity is much more productive than hostile aggression. Have a good time teaching and expect your students to enjoy coming to class and playing tennis. Make learning fun, even if it requires hard work. Do not tolerate pouting, sad faces, or negative self-talk.

KEEPING SCORE

The participant's book (*Tennis: Steps to Success*, Step 7) has a series of questions about keeping score. Following are alternate questions on the same topic.

Scoring Quiz

Directions: Write *T* (True) or *F* (False) in the blank provided.

_____ 1. A total of 4 points is played in a game using no-ad scoring.

_____ 2. When the score is 2–1, the server serves from the left side of the baseline.

_____ 3. When the score is 3–3 in a no-ad game, the receiver determines from which side the server serves.

_____ 4. In conventional scoring the score is 0–30 if the server wins the first 2 points.

_____ 5. In conventional scoring the receiver is leading when the score is 30–40.

_____ 6. In conventional scoring the score is 40–0 if the server wins the first 3 points.

_____ 7. In conventional scoring the score is 40–15 if the server has won 3 of the first 4 points.

_____ 8. In conventional scoring the score is deuce if both players have won 2 points.

_____ 9. In conventional scoring the game is over if the server loses 1 more point when the score is 40–30.

_____ 10. *Ad in* means the server can win the game if he or she wins the next point.

_____ 11. *Ad out* means the receiver is ahead by 1 point after a deuce score.

_____ 12. The minimum number of points in a complete game is 5.

_____ 13. The maximum number of games that can be played before a tiebreaker is 12.

_____ 14. A player who wins a pro set wins the match.

_____ 15. A player must win at least 7 points to win a tiebreaker.

_____ 16. The player who served the previous game serves first in a tiebreaker.

_____ 17. The server stands on the right side to serve the first point of a tiebreaker.

_____ 18. The third point of a tiebreaker is served from the right side.

_____ 19. During a tiebreaker the players change ends of the court every 6 points.

_____ 20. After a tiebreaker the players remain on their respective sides to begin the next set.

_____ 21. During a set the players change ends of the court whenever the total number of games played is an odd number.

_____ 22. The receiver is responsible for calling out the score before each point.

_____ 23. If the set score is 4–2, the set has been completed.

_____ 24. When players split sets, the order of serving that has been established continues in the third set.

_____ 25. With set scores of 6–3, 7–5, a two out of three set match has been completed.

Scoring Quiz Answers

1. False
2. True
3. True
4. False
5. True
6. True
7. True
8. False
9. False
10. True
11. True
12. False
13. True
14. True
15. True
16. False
17. True
18. True
19. True
20. False
21. True
22. False
23. False
24. True
25. True

If your schedule permits, allow your students opportunities in class to play points, games, sets, and tiebreakers in order to get practice keeping score. When there is an odd number of players on the courts, those not playing can serve as scorekeepers.

Step 8   Beginner's Volley

The volley is often one of the last strokes a developing tennis player learns to perfect. Although most players are taught to hit a volley early in their instruction progression, using a Continental grip effectively usually comes later. As a result, you will see people in your class who demonstrate good technique on groundstrokes but still look like beginners when they get to the net. This will make the job of identifying levels of ability more difficult, but recognizing the characteristics described soon will help.

There is disagreement among teachers and pros about the proper grip for beginners to use with the volley. Some teach a forehand grip for forehand volleys, with a change to the backhand for shots on the opposite side. Changing grips, they believe, allows players to be comfortable with grips on both sides of the body. There will be time later to convert to a Continental grip.

Others, however, believe that the Continental grip should be taught from the beginning. Although this grip is more difficult to learn, those who can use it will have an advantage as their games move up to higher levels.

Most of the problems players have at the net are simply a matter of not being used to playing in that position. Some people are afraid of getting hit with the ball, others do not feel they are quick enough to make contact with the ball, and others just play better with time to prepare for groundstrokes. The solution for all three groups is to get them to the net as much as possible. The more times a person is put into a situation, the more comfortable and efficient this person will be.

STUDENT KEYS TO SUCCESS

- Start in ready position
- Use short backswing
- Change grips if necessary
- Step forward
- Hit out to side
- Recover quickly

Beginner's Volley Rating

CHECKPOINT	BEGINNING LEVEL	INTERMEDIATE LEVEL	ADVANCED LEVEL
Preparation	• Avoids the net • Holds a frying pan grip	• Exaggerates back-swing • Holds a forehand grip	• Not applicable
Swing	• May miss the ball • Hits only forehand volleys • Cannot direct shots • Racket turns in hand	• Makes contact • May try backhand volleys • Hits backhand with forehand grip • Can direct ball, but accurate pace and direction are difficult	

Beginner's Volley Rating

CHECKPOINT	BEGINNING LEVEL	INTERMEDIATE LEVEL	ADVANCED LEVEL
Follow-Through	• None	• Makes complete swing but may not recover quickly for next shot	

Error Detection and Correction for Beginner's Volley

Expect to see wholesale errors when beginners and intermediates play at the net. The problems of not having as much time to react, of changing the length of the backswing, and of having to cope with grip changes are very difficult for most inexperienced players. As teacher, concentrate on one small problem or correction at a time. Trying to fix everything that breaks down at the net at once is impossible. At times, it is better to overlook some faults in order to correct others.

ERROR

CORRECTION

ERROR	CORRECTION
1. Student shows reluctance to play at the net.	1. Familiarity will solve this problem. The more time spent at the net, the more comfortable the player will become. Look for opportunities in practice for student to play at the net. He or she could play games in which points won with volleys are scored as 2 points.

ERROR   **CORRECTION**

2. Student gets too close to the ball.

2. Set up shots that force the student to move. Toss balls directly at the player's face and make him or her step to the side. Tell players who get too close to the ball to try to hit it with the tip end of the racket head.

3. Student exhibits excessive backswing.

3. Have player stand with back to a wall or a fence to restrict the backswing before he or she returns tossed balls. Also try having the player hold the racket out in front of the body with the racket touching the net. Then hit shots for the player to volley. With the racket starting on the net, there will not be time for a big backswing.

ERROR 🚫

CORRECTION

4. Student has a loose grip.

4. Tell the student to hold tightly and hit the racket with the off hand to check the firmness of the grip.

5. Student has no forward pivot.

5. Position the player between two objects or in a corner of the court where the fence forms a right angle. Toss balls to the player so that he or she has to step forward to hit the shot without touching the objects or the fence.

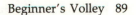

ERROR

CORRECTION

6. Student has a droopy wrist.

6. Have your student keep the racket head higher than the wrist. The shaft of the racket and the forearm should nearly form a 90-degree angle. Discourage the two-handed backhand at the net; it is very difficult to get the ball up and over the net when the racket head starts as low as it does with the two-handed grip.

Beginner's Volley Drills

1. Toss to Volley
[Corresponds to *Tennis*, Step 8, Drill 3]

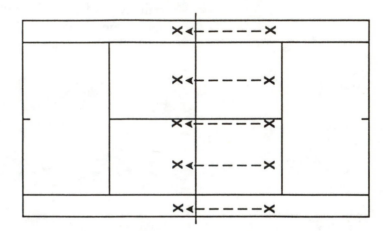

Group Management and Safety Tips

- Put 8 to 10 players on each court.
- Spread the players along the length of the net, far enough apart to avoid touching rackets.
- The remainder of the court can be used for the same basic activity, but with no net. Rotate positions so that every player gets a turn at the net.
- Tossers use an underhand motion.

Equipment

- Balls, 3 per student pair

Instructions to Class

- ''Have a partner stand about 20 feet on the opposite side of the net. Your partner tosses balls to your forehand, to your backhand, and directly at you, but not in any particular order, so be ready for any shot. Bump the ball back to your partner, who catches and tosses without using a racket.''

Student Option

- ''Count the number of consecutive volleys you return so accurately that your partner does not have to move to catch the ball.''

Student Success Goal

- 10 of 15 volleys back to the tosser

To Decrease Difficulty

- Decrease the distance between volleyer and tosser, who tosses softly.
- Have feeder toss only to the forehand side, then only to the backhand side.
- Reduce the Success Goal to 5 of 15.

To Increase Difficulty

- Increase the distance between tosser and volleyer.
- Have the tosser increase the pace of the balls being fed to the volleyer.
- Increase the Success Goal to 12 of 15.

2. Back-to-the-Wall Volleys
[Corresponds to *Tennis*, Step 8, Drill 4]

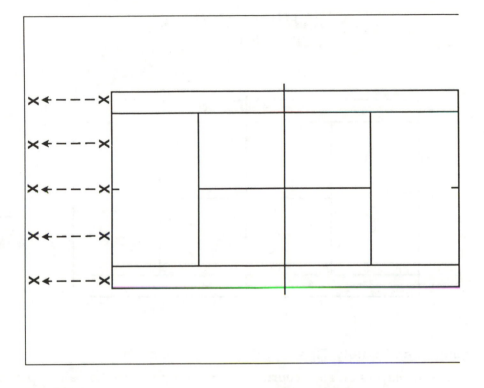

Group Management and Safety Tips

- Put 10 to 20 players on each court, separating pairs of players by 8 to 10 feet.
- Pair players by ability at first. Then place stronger players with weaker ones so the stronger can help the weaker both by tossing correctly and by bumping volleys back accurately.
- With each pair, use a third player to retrieve balls. Have this one rotate in as a tosser or a hitter.
- Emphasize bumping the ball back to the tosser, not swinging and hitting.

Equipment

- Balls, 2 per student pair

Instructions to Class

- "Stand with your back against a fence or wall. Your partner stands about 20 feet away and tosses balls, which you return with volleys. Move forward quickly when the ball approaches, stepping forward with the foot on the side opposite the ball. Switch positions after 20 tosses."

Student Options

- "Request tosses directed to your weaker side."
- "Request a variety of paces and directions."
- "Compete with your partner for more consecutive returns."

Student Success Goal

- 20 consecutive volleys without touching the racket to the fence or wall

To Decrease Difficulty

- Decrease the distance between the tosser and the volleyer.
- Have the tosser toss only to the forehand side, then only to the backhand side.
- Allow the volleyer to start with the racket to the side.

To Increase Difficulty

- Increase the distance between the tosser and the volleyer.
- Have the tosser mix the feeds between the forehand and the backhand sides.

3. Hit to Volleys
[New drill]

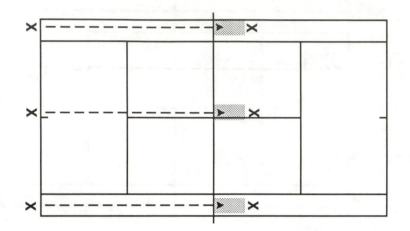

Group Management and Safety Tips

- Put three pairs of players on each court.
- Use four more players per court to retrieve balls. They rotate to hit or toss.
- Players rotate every 2 minutes or every 30 shots.

Equipment

- Balls, 3 per student pair

Instructions to Class

- "Stand at the net opposite a partner at the service line or baseline. Your partner will drop and hit balls to your forehand and backhand sides. Return each setup with a volley, then recover for the next setup. Don't worry about exact placement now; just make contact and get the ball back in the general direction of the feeder. Practicing controlled volleys now will enable you to place shots away from your opponent later."

Student Option

- "Try to keep the ball in play with your volleys and your partner's groundstrokes."

Student Success Goal

- 15 of 30 volleys

To Decrease Difficulty

- Decrease the distance between the hitter and the volleyer. Have the feeder set up with softer shots.
- Reduce the Success Goal to 10 of 30.
- Have feeder set up balls only to the forehand, then only to the backhand.
- Use better player to set up shots for weaker player.

To Increase Difficulty

- Have the feeder increase pace of setup shots.
- Have feeder mix setups between the forehand and the backhand.
- Increase the Success Goal to 20 of 30.

4. Cage Drill
[New drill]

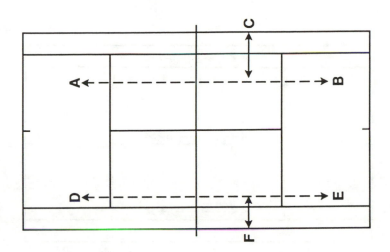

Group Management and Safety Tips

- Put six players on each court.
- Use additional players to retrieve balls, then to enter the rotations.

Equipment

- Balls, at least 3 per student trio

Instructions to Class

- "Get into groups of three. Two players stand just behind opposite service lines and hit soft groundstrokes while the third player stays off to the side of the net 'in a cage.' This third player moves out of the cage every other shot to bump a volley back to the player on the opposite side of the net. The volleyer should hit, get out of the way, let a shot pass the net, then move back to volley again."

Student Option

- "Count the number of consecutive hits your team makes without an error."

Student Success Goal

- 9 consecutive shots from the three team members

To Decrease Difficulty

- Reduce the Success Goal to 8, 7, or 6.
- Have players decrease the pace of the groundstrokes.

To Increase Difficulty

- Increase the Success Goal by increments of 3.
- Increase the distance between players hitting groundstrokes.

5. *Consecutive Volleys*
[Corresponds to *Tennis*, Step 8, Drill 5]

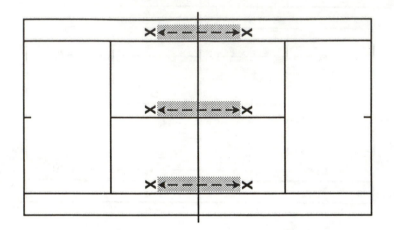

Group Management and Safety Tips

- Put six players on each court.
- Use other players to retrieve balls, then rotate in.
- Pair stronger and weaker players together to stabilize the drill.
- Encourage players to bump the ball instead of swinging and hitting.
- Only advanced beginners will have success with this drill.

Equipment

- Balls, at least 3 per student pair

Instructions to Class

- "Stand about 15 feet from the net; keep a ball in play hitting volleys with a partner an equal distance on the opposite side of the net. Bump the ball without much pace. Recover quickly for the next shot. Keep your racket up and in front of your body."

Student Options

- "Set team goals."
- "Change the distance between you and your partner."

Student Success Goal

- 6 consecutive volleys

To Decrease Difficulty

- Reduce the Success Goal to 4.
- Place a stronger player with a weaker player to stabilize the drill.

To Increase Difficulty

- Increase the Success Goal by increments of 2.
- Increase the distance between players.
- Have players increase the pace of shots.

6. *"Umpiring" Drill*
[New drill]

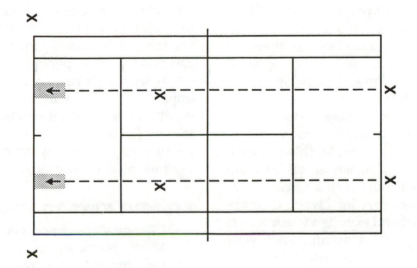

Group Management and Safety Tips

- Put two pairs of players on each court.
- Use a third player to serve as a line judge for each pair.

Equipment

- Balls, 1 basket per court

Instructions to Class

- "Stand in a volleying position about 12 feet from the net. Have a partner hit a variety of shots that land inside, on, or just outside the baseline. Instead of volleying, call shots "in" or "out" as they fly by you, then turn quickly to see whether you are predicting their distances correctly. Learn to decide quickly whether or not to play shots that would land close to the baseline."

Student Options

- "Set personal goals."
- "Change positions every time you miss a line call."
- "Make it a judging contest between you and your practice partner."

Student Success Goal

- 10 consecutive correct calls

To Decrease Difficulty

- Have hitter reduce the pace of shots.
- Reduce the Success Goal to 8, 6, or 4 consecutive correct calls.

To Increase Difficulty

- Have hitter increase the pace of shots.
- Increase the Success Goal by increments of 2.

Step 9 Lob

Beginners hit more lobs accidentally than on purpose. Intermediates begin to realize the possibilities of lobbing, but don't do it very effectively. Advanced players use the lob as a defensive ploy and as an offensive weapon. The lob is difficult to teach because there are very few drills that can simulate game situations. As players mature, they begin to find situations in which they can use the lob. Then they practice the shot during matches.

Tell your students to use the lob as a defensive shot to get out of trouble, that is, when the opponent hits a smash or drives them deep into the backcourt with a forcing shot. On offense, they can try lobs when their opponent is at the net and expects a passing shot. Instead of giving him or her that shot, your students can hit a low offensive lob for a winner.

After players have learned what a lob is, they sometimes use it too much. There is a great temptation to automatically go to the lob when in doubt or under a little pressure. Try to teach players to trust the strokes they practice most often, usually the forehand and the backhand. If the opponent knows a player will lob every time a certain situation exists, the opponent can move into position to win the point with a smash. It will be relatively easy for you to identify your students' skill levels because you really only have to worry about the intermediate and advanced players.

STUDENT KEYS TO SUCCESS

- Change grips if necessary
- Move, plant, and swing
- Use low-to-high swing
- Hit through the shot

Lob Rating

CHECKPOINT	BEGINNING LEVEL	INTERMEDIATE LEVEL	ADVANCED LEVEL
Preparation	• Not applicable	• May not be in proper position with feet • Backswing erratic	• Moves quickly to position to lob • Backswing full when in control, short when in trouble
Swing		• Uses the shot only when in trouble • Tries to fight power with power • Frequently lobs short	• Full swing when necessary • Can block ball to stay in point
Follow-Through		• May be incomplete	• Full, sweeping motion on offensive lobs • Moves to anticipate next shot

Error Detection and Correction for the Lob

Watch for good results rather than technique on lobs. If something goes wrong with the stroke, look for position of the feet first, then check the other "Keys to Success" (see Figure 9.1 in *Tennis: Steps to Success*). There is a temptation for many players to fight the power of an oncoming smash with their own power. When returning smashes, one should use the velocity of the other player's shot as much as possible. Many times a simple block while the racket is held tightly will propel the ball back into the opposite backcourt.

ERROR 🚫

CORRECTION

ERROR	CORRECTION
1. Student underhits, hitting shallow lobs.	1. Have your student practice hitting to targets in the backcourt area. Any mistakes should be deep, not short. Shots should peak in height beyond the net and land as near the baseline as possible. Remind your student to follow through after the hit for more depth.
2. Student overhits, hitting lobs beyond the baseline.	2. Tell your student to resist the temptation to fight power with power. Alternately feed hard and soft shots to the lobber so he or she can get used to putting the required amount of speed on the lob.
3. There is a low trajectory on the lob.	3. Have your student work on a low-to-high swing, starting the swing with the racket touching the ground. Your student should aim for the baseline instead of just trying to clear the volleyer's racket, especially on defensive lobs.

Lob Drills

1. *Drop-and-Hit Lobs*
[Corresponds to *Tennis*, Step 9, Drill 1]

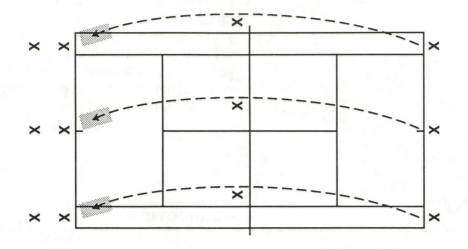

Group Management and Safety Tips

- Put six to nine players on each court.
- Rotate players from one position to the next in sequence.
- Use waiting players to retrieve balls.

Equipment

- Balls, at least 3 per student trio

Instructions to Class

- ''Stand behind the baseline. Drop and hit forehand and backhand lobs over the outstretched racket of a practice partner standing at the net; the lobs should go into the opposite backcourt. Depending on whether your opponent is right-handed or left-handed, place your lobs to the appropriate backhand corner.''

Student Option

- Not applicable

Student Success Goal

- 10 of 15 lobs hit into the backcourt area

To Decrease Difficulty

- Have the lobber hit forehand lobs only.
- Remove the player at the net.
- Reduce the Success Goal to 5 of 15.

To Increase Difficulty

- Allow player at the net to play the shot when the lob is too low or short.

2. *Lob Rally*
[New drill]

Group Management and Safety Tips

- Put two or four players on each court.
- With four players, use corner-to-corner lob patterns, with two pairs of players keeping two balls in play simultaneously.

Equipment

- Balls, at least 3 per student pair

Instructions to Class

- ''Two practice partners stand behind the baselines in opposite corners of the court. Either player can drop a ball and put it into play with a lob. Then both keep the ball going using only lobs. Remember to make any mistakes deep, lift the ball with your racket, and follow through in the direction you are hitting.''

Student Option

- ''Compete against opponents in 5-point games.''

Student Success Goal

- 6 consecutive lobs

To Decrease Difficulty

- Put only two players on a court at a time to allow more room for maneuvering along the baseline.

To Increase Difficulty

- Make a line 10 feet inside the baseline and require that every lob must bounce between that line and the baseline.

3. *Run and Lob*
[Corresponds to *Tennis*, Step 9, Drill 2]

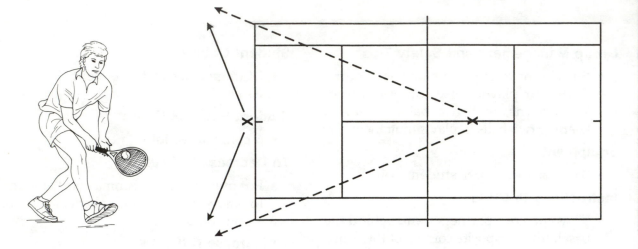

Group Management and Safety Tips
- This drill may not be appropriate for large classes.
- Put two players on a court at a time.

Equipment
- Balls, at least 3 per student pair

Instructions to Class
- "Your partner stands at the net and alternates driving shots to your forehand and your backhand corners. Move to the ball and return with lobs. Remember to lob crosscourt when pulled off deep into a corner of the court. If you are feeding, drive shots that bounce high and deep into either corner. Time your feeds so they are difficult but not impossible to run down and return."

Student Option
- "Play out the point."

Student Success Goal
- 10 of 20 lobs into the backcourt area

To Decrease Difficulty
- Have the feeder set up shots nearer the center of the court, at the service line, but still deep enough to force a lob.
- Have the feeder set up shots with less pace.
- Decrease the Success Goal to 5 of 20.

To Increase Difficulty
- Have feeder increase pace on setups.
- Have feeder set up shots farther into the corners.
- Increase the Success Goal to 15 of 20.

4. 2-on-2 Lob-Drive Drill
[New drill]

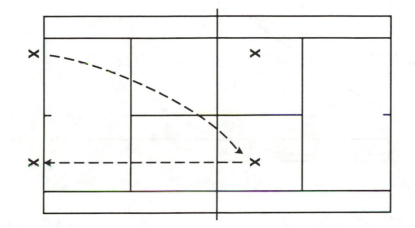

Group Management and Safety Tips

- Put four players on each court.
- This drill is more appropriate for better players.

Equipment

- Balls, at least 3 per court

Instructions to Class

- "Two players stand behind the baseline; one puts the ball into play with a lob to either of two players at the net. Play the point out, using lobs and smashes, if volleyers can hit smashes. If not, they can let the ball bounce, then drive the ball deeply into the backcourt. If you are lobbing and the ball comes directly toward you, take a short backswing and block the ball. If you have to run for the ball, take enough backswing to lift the ball high and deep into the backcourt. Then scramble back to a central position to retrieve the next shot."

Student Option

- "Compete against opponents in 5-point games."

Student Success Goal

- Win at least half of the games played.

To Decrease Difficulty

- Place the strongest players in the baseline positions.
- Score 2 points for every winning lob.

To Increase Difficulty

- Require player at the net to hit controlled smashes instead of winners.

5. *Corner to Corner*
[New drill]

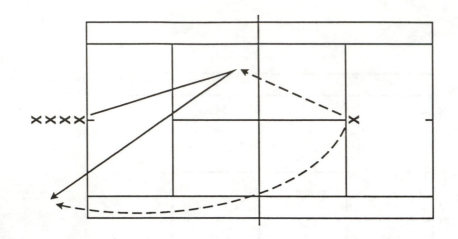

Group Management and Safety Tips

- Put four to eight players on each court.
- Only players skilled at setting up shots can work as feeders.
- Have feeders change the pattern by hitting first to the forehand, then to the backhand corners.
- Require players to let the balls bounce before returning them.

Equipment

- Balls, 1 basket per court

Instructions to Class

- ''Form a line behind the center mark on the court. The feeder will hit a shot just over the net to your backhand, then will immediately lob to the opposite corner. Run forward, get the short shot back, then turn and run to retrieve the second ball with a lob. Because you will be moving away from the court on the second shot, take a strong, full swing to compensate for the lack of power. Then move to the end of the line to wait for another turn.''

Student Option

- ''Direct both returns to target areas on the court.''

Student Success Goal

- 6 consecutive shots returned to the singles court

To Decrease Difficulty

- Have feeder set up player with softer, closer shots.

To Increase Difficulty

- Increase the Success Goal by increments of 2.
- Have the feeder set the second shot deeper into the corner.

Step 10   Smash

The smash is one of the shots that distinguishes beginners from intermediate and advanced players. Beginners don't have a smash simply because no one has taught them how to hit one. Intermediates use the smash but may not use it at the right time, at the right place on the court, or with the correct technique.

Your role as instructor is to introduce this stroke to beginning players, to help intermediates develop the smash into a reliable, point-winning stroke, and to give advanced players enough practice to keep their smashes in good working order. From the standpoint of the time available in a tennis class, the smash is difficult to teach. It almost has to be a one-on-one situation between you and the student because very few students are good enough to set the ball properly with lobs. As a safety consideration, smashes being hit on multiple courts present a hazard to those not actively participating in the drills.

The smash is one stroke in which the player can swing hard, hit hard, and try to crush the ball. Teach that if the lob is short and the smasher is in good body and court position to hit a winner, a player should go for the winner with a flat, high-bouncing smash. If the player is out of position, off balance, or deep in the backcourt, he or she should use the controlled smash; the player should hit a controlled spin smash to an open area of the court, then follow it to the net to finish the point.

Whatever your students do, don't let them wait for a high-bouncing lob to bounce up and get back down to waist level. Instead, have them step under the ball after the bounce and hit a smash. Watch for the following characteristics to determine intermediate- or advanced-level smashes. It is probably best to wait for beginners to become advanced beginners or intermediates before introducing the smash. The shot requires a sense of timing that few players have until spending several weeks on the court.

STUDENT KEYS TO SUCCESS

- Move feet into position
- Use Continental grip
- Pull racket back early
- Reach high to hit

Smash Rating

CHECKPOINT	BEGINNING LEVEL	INTERMEDIATE LEVEL	ADVANCED LEVEL
Preparation	• Not applicable	• Sluggish footwork • May hold forehand grip • Takes full back-swing	• Takes many small steps to get into position • Uses Continental grip • Immediately draws racket to backscratch position

Smash Rating

CHECKPOINT	BEGINNING LEVEL	INTERMEDIATE LEVEL	ADVANCED LEVEL
Swing		• Can hit smashes within reach • May let ball drop too low before hitting • May lose points trying to overhit	• Extends arm on contact • Can direct shots • Can hit off balance • Can hit flat or spin smashes
Follow-Through		• May cross body too soon with racket	• Finishes on either side of body with racket, depending on situation

Error Detection and Correction for Smash

Although the action for this shot takes place high over the player's head, keep your eyes on the feet. Watch for the smasher's taking short, quick steps to get into position. The rest of the shot usually falls into place if the feet are where they belong before the swing is made. If you can concentrate on technique early in teaching the smash, adding power will come naturally as the student gets stronger and develops the timing necessary to generate that power.

ERROR

1. Student uses an excessive windup.

2. Student uses a forehand grip.

3. Student has poor footwork.

CORRECTION

1. Make the hitter immediately cock the racket back behind the head. Too much racket motion causes errors. The student should draw back the racket like a quarterback bringing back a football before making a pass.

2. Although this grip works on some smashes, the ball tends to fly on others. Make your student try the Continental grip. The student should keep the ball slightly out to the side of the body when preparing to hit.

3. Demand many short preparation steps as the hitter turns the nonhitting side to the net. If the ball goes deep, retreating with this side to the net is better than backpedaling while facing the net.

ERROR 🚫

CORRECTION

4. Student lets the ball drop too low.

4. Have your student extend the arm and body to hit, reaching for the sky. Contact should be made as high as possible. Some teachers tell students to point to the ball with the opposite hand, then to swing in the direction the hand is pointing.

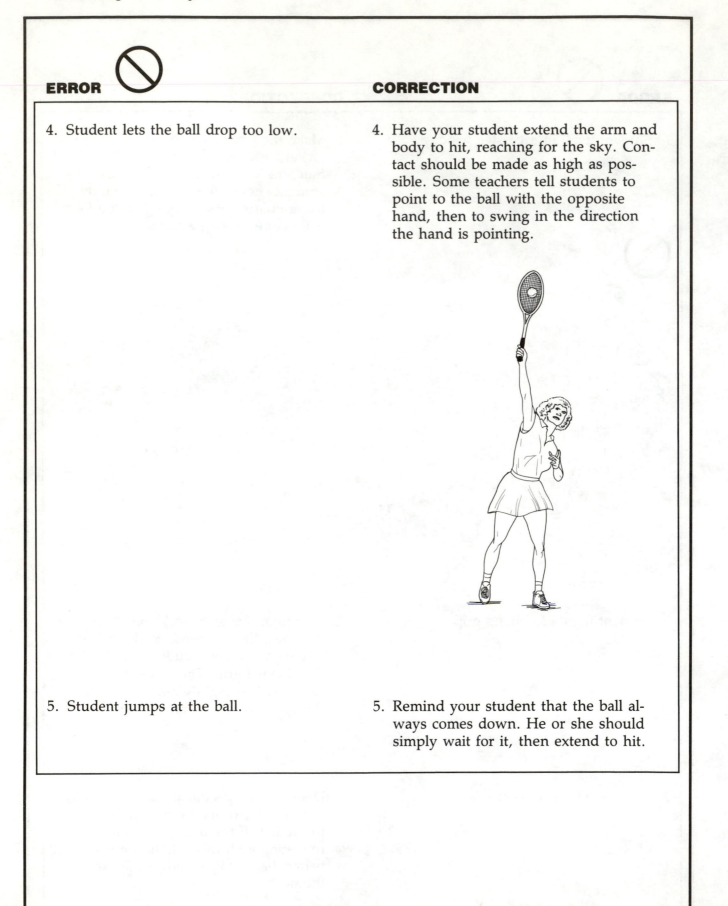

5. Student jumps at the ball.

5. Remind your student that the ball always comes down. He or she should simply wait for it, then extend to hit.

ERROR

6. Student faces the net while hitting.

CORRECTION

6. Have your student keep the nonhitting shoulder toward the net until the last moment, then rotate the upper body with the swing.

Smash Drills

1. Slap the Net
[New drill]

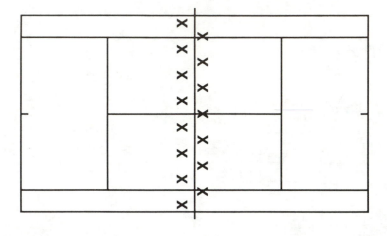

Group Management and Safety Tips

- Put up to fifteen players on each court.
- Position players along the length of the net on both sides, then alternate groups simulating the swing.
- Demonstrate the wrist pronation by catching your forearm as you swing.
- Have each player swing at least 10 times.

Equipment

- Rackets, 1 per student

Instructions to Class

- "Take a position within 3 or 4 feet from the net. Start with your racket in a back-scratch position. On command, reach high, simulate a smash, and slap the net, with both edges of the racket frame hitting it simultaneously. Strike the net so that it makes a popping sound when the frame hits it. Swing through the overhead motion and hit the net 10 times."

Student Option

- "Visualize yourself extending your body to hit, then make a popping sound with the racket hitting the net. It won't hurt your racket."

Student Success Goal

- 10 swings and net slaps

To Decrease Difficulty

- Let the student slow down the swing motion.

To Increase Difficulty

- Have player swing with eyes closed.

2. Point and Catch
[New drill]

Group Management and Safety Tips

- Put four players on each court.
- Separate the pairs on each court, using alleys for extra space.

Equipment

- Balls, 3 per student pair

Instructions to Class

- ''Take a position about 10 feet from the net. A partner on the other side hits or tosses lobs. Draw the racket back with your strong arm and point to the ball with your opposite hand. Point to exactly the place where you would make contact if you were to hit the ball. Instead of hitting a smash, though, catch the ball with the pointing hand extended high and in front of your position.''

Student Option

- ''Compete with your partner for more consecutive catches.''

Student Success Goal

- 10 consecutive catches

To Decrease Difficulty

- Have the feeder lob or toss lower and softer setups.
- Position both players closer to the net.
- Reduce the Success Goal to 5.

To Increase Difficulty

- Increase the distance from the net for both players.
- Have the feeder increase the height of setups.
- Increase the Success Goal by increments of 2.

3. Setup Smashes
[New drill]

Group Management and Safety Tips

- Put two or four players on each court.
- Use both sides of the court and two balls simultaneously if four players are on the court.
- Setting up players with well-placed lobs is difficult. More experienced players may have to be used as setters.
- Warn players to keep eyes open for stray shots. Also, they should warn others when errant shots are hit.

Equipment

- Balls, at least 3 per student pair

Instructions to Class

- ''Take a position 8 to 10 feet from the net. Your partner sets you up with low, soft lobs. Reach high to hit; attempt to hit controlled smashes back in the direction of your practice partner. Get your racket back early and make contact in front of your body.''

Student Option

- Not applicable

Student Success Goal

- Make contact with the ball on 8 of 10 smash attempts.

To Decrease Difficulty

- Move the player hitting smashes closer to the net.
- Have the smasher start with the racket in the backscratch position.

To Increase Difficulty

- Move the player hitting smashes farther from the net.
- Have the feeder increase the height of lobs to require better timing.

4. Smash and Touch
[Corresponds to *Tennis*, Step 10, Drill 3]

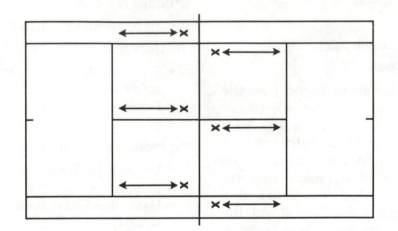

Group Management and Safety Tips

- Put two to six players on each court before they rotate.
- Try to keep all players moving back, then forward, simultaneously.
- This is a good drill with which to finish a class period.

Equipment

- Rackets, 1 per student

Instructions to Class

- "Start within a racket's length of the net. Move back and, with no ball involved, swing through the entire smash motion, carrying forward to touch the net. Remember to turn your side as you move back to hit; you should be looking over your shoulder to follow the ball. Repeat the sequence 10 times before rotating with another player."

Student Option

- "Have a partner feed lobs so you can actually smash a ball before touching the net with the racket."

Student Success Goal

- 10 consecutive simulated smashes and net touches

To Decrease Difficulty

- Reduce the Success Goal.

To Increase Difficulty

- Increase the Success Goal by increments of 5.
- Require player to actually hit smashes rather than simulate the shot.

5. *Lob-Smash Combination*
[Corresponds to *Tennis*, Step 10, Drill 4]

Group Management and Safety Tips

- Put two players on each court, if class size permits.
- Have waiting players stand clear of the baseline area.
- For safety reasons, put no more than four players on each court.

Equipment

- Balls, at least 3 per student pair

Instructions to Class

- ''Have a partner hit lobs from the baseline to you at the net. Return the lobs with controlled smashes. Move your feet with quick, short steps as you prepare to hit. Get the racket back immediately into the backscratch position; don't take a full windup. Hit 10 smashes before rotating.''

Student Option

- ''Play the points out and keep score.''

Student Success Goal

- 10 controlled smashes placed into the singles court

To Decrease Difficulty

- Position the smasher closer to the net.
- Reduce the Success Goal to 10 attempts instead of 10 good smashes.

To Increase Difficulty

- Increase the Success Goal to 15 good smashes.
- Position the smasher farther from the net.

6. Smash to Target
[Corresponds to *Tennis*, Step 10, Drill 5]

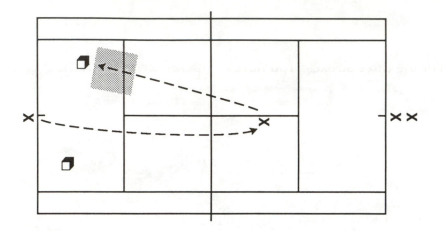

Group Management and Safety Tips

- Put two players on each court, one hitting smashes, one feeding lobs.
- Alert the waiting players to watch for balls being smashed.
- This drill will work only with players able to hit controlled smashes.

Equipment

- Balls, at least 3 per student pair
- Cones, towels, boxes, or tennis cans for targets

Instructions to Class

- ''Your partner hits lobs from the baseline to you at the net. Return the lobs with smashes directed at targets (or target areas) on the court. Hit the ball solidly without trying to swing as hard as possible. A controlled smash can win points as often as a smash hit with 100 percent velocity. Attempt 10 smashes before rotating.''

Student Option

- Keep score and compete against yourself or a partner.

Student Success Goal

- 5 of 10 smashes hit to the target area

To Decrease Difficulty

- Reduce the Success Goal to 3 of 10.
- Position smasher closer to the net.

To Increase Difficulty

- Increase the Success Goal to 6 of 10.
- Position players farther from the net.

Step 11   Volley–Lob–Smash Combinations

At this point your students have been introduced to the volley, the lob, and the smash. Now it is your responsibility to give them as much time as is practical for trying various combinations of the three strokes. You have a good idea of the ability levels of your students, so now focus on movement, transition between strokes, and using the shots in game situations. One way to encourage these strokes is to have students play games in which they are rewarded if a point is won using a volley, a lob, or a smash. When this happens, 2 points can be given to the hitter instead of 1, or the game can be declared over with a winning volley, lob, or smash.

Volley–Lob–Smash Combination Drills

1. *Up and Back*
[Corresponds to *Tennis*, Step 11, Drill 1]

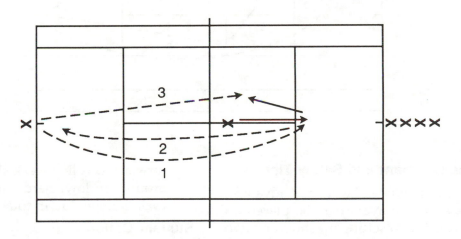

Group Management and Safety Tips

- Put two players on each court.
- Keep other players well behind the baseline before their turns.
- The drill will work only with a player at the baseline who can hit controlled lobs and drives.

Equipment

- Balls, 1 basket per court

Instructions to Class

- ''Have a partner stand at the baseline with a basket of balls. You start about 10 feet from the net, then move back to smash a lob fed to you by your partner. As soon as you hit the smash, move forward to volley a short drive set up by your partner (with a separate ball). Don't wait to see where your smash goes; immediately follow it to the net for the next shot. Continue this sequence for 10 smashes and 10 volleys.''

Student Options

- "Set personal goals."
- "Compete with your partner for more shots hit into the singles court."

Student Success Goal

- 10 of 20 smashes and volleys hit into the singles court

To Decrease Difficulty

- Reduce the Success Goal to 8 or 6 of 20 attempts.
- Have the feeder set up lobs closer to the net and lower.

To Increase Difficulty

- Increase the Success Goal by increments of 2.

2. Volley-Volley-Smash

[Corresponds to *Tennis*, Step 11, Drill 3]

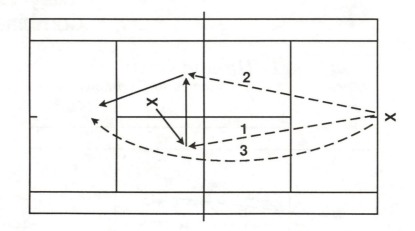

Group Management and Safety Tips

- With intermediate players and advanced players, four players may be placed on each court: two setting up shots and two volleying and smashing. Each pair uses half of the court.

Equipment

- Balls, 1 basket per court

Instructions to Class

- "Start at the net against a partner at the baseline with a basket of balls. Your partner sets you up for a forehand volley, then a backhand volley, then back for a smash. The partner setting up shots does not return the volleys but uses 3 balls. Move forward to volley weak shots; hold your ground on low, hard shots. Repeat the cycle 5 times for 15 total shots."

Student Option

- Not applicable

Student Success Goal

- 10 of 15 returns

To Decrease Difficulty

- Reduce the Success Goal to 8 or 6 of 15 returns.

To Increase Difficulty

- Increase the Success Goal by increments of 2.

3. *Three-on-One Lobs and Volleys*
[New drill]

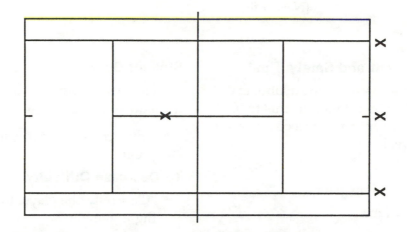

Group Management and Safety Tips

- Put four players on each court.
- Alert the waiting players to stay clear of the court.

Equipment

- Balls, 1 basket per court

Instructions to Class

- ''Three players stand at one baseline with a basket of balls. They are opposed by only one player at the net on the opposite side. Any of the three players puts a ball into play with a lob; the player at the net returns it with a smash. The point is played out using only lobs and smashes. Any of the three lobbing players may return a smash. If you are smashing, try to move the ball around the court into open spaces. If you are returning smashes, try to anticipate where the smash will go by watching how the smasher sets his or her feet and by watching the racket face at contact. Rotate after either the sole player or the three-person team wins 5 points. Alleys are in play for shots hit by the player smashing; however, that player defends only the singles court.''

Student Option

- ''Work on direction and pace as well as technique.''

Student Success Goal

- Win at least one game while hitting smashes.

To Decrease Difficulty

- Have lobbers lob closer to the net and lower.
- Have students practice technique rather than keep score.

To Increase Difficulty

- Require the player at the net to start from a deeper position.
- Reduce the number of players at the baseline to two to make the drill harder for them.

4. *Volleys and Smashes Win*
[New drill]

Group Management and Safety Tips

- Coach students on when to advance to the net. There is a temptation in this type of game to move into the forecourt, even following weak shots.

Equipment

- Balls, 3 per student pair

Instructions to Class

- "Play 4-point games against a partner. A game is won immediately if one of you hits a winning volley or smash. Don't become so eager to get to the net that you advance after hitting weak shots. Select the right time to move in, when your opponent is in trouble or deep behind the baseline."

Student Option

- Not applicable

Student Success Goal

- Advance to the net on at least every other point.

To Decrease Difficulty

- Allow only one player to go to the net during a game.

To Increase Difficulty

- Take points away if a volley, a lob, or a smash is missed.

5. Series Drill
[New drill]

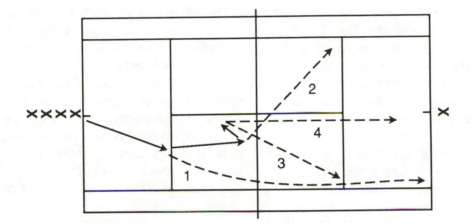

Group Management and Safety Tips

- Put six to eight players on each court.
- Rotate players out to retrieve balls.
- Keep the court clear of balls.
- Repeat the drill enough times for players to get into a groove with the strokes being practiced.

Equipment

- Balls, 1 basket per court

Instructions to Class

- "Line up behind the center mark of the baseline. A feeder will set you up with a short shot to your forehand. Move in, hit the ball down the line closer to your position on the court (1), and go to the end of the line behind the baseline. On successive rounds, the feeder will setup a forehand volley (2), then a backhand volley (3), then an overhead smash (4). Try for a perfect series, every shot going into the singles court to set you up for winners."

Student Option

- "Play out the point after the smash."

Student Success Goal

- A perfect series of 4 consecutive in shots

To Decrease Difficulty

- Have the feeder hit softer shots.

To Increase Difficulty

- Have the feeder hit shots with more pace and range.
- Move player down a court or make him or her pick up balls with two or more misses in the same series. The added pressure will simulate game situations and will improve concentration.

Step 12 Advanced Volley

As this shot's name implies, only advanced players can use the advanced volley. The distinguishing characteristic of this stroke is the use of the Continental grip, with the wrist directly over the top part of the handle. This contrasts with changing between a forehand and backhand grip, depending on where the ball is hit.

In advanced levels of tennis, there is simply not enough time to change grips at the net with every shot. Some advanced players attempt to change grips or to hold the racket with either a forehand or backhand grip, but they run a high risk of getting caught between grips or of hitting without enough power to win points outright at the net. The Continental grip may not feel as comfortable as either other grip, but it is the best compromise available for power and control. With players who insist on trying to change between the forehand and backhand grips, consider it an opportunity to make them even more effective by your teaching them the Continental grip.

The advanced volley is a good indicator of a player's aggressiveness. Try to instill the idea that after a good volley, one should move a bit closer to the net for a winner. Some players hit a good shot, then stand there admiring that shot while getting passed by a better return. At the net the volleyer can see a huge amount of the opponent's court open for angled winners. Hitting volleys is not the time to be tentative; if a player gets to the net, it is time for the point to be won on the first or second volley.

STUDENT KEYS TO SUCCESS

- Hold Continental grip tightly
- Be ready for action
- Move forward to hit
- Make contact early
- Hit through the shot
- Recover quickly

Advanced Volley Rating

CHECKPOINT	BEGINNING LEVEL	INTERMEDIATE LEVEL	ADVANCED LEVEL
Preparation	• Not applicable	• Not applicable	• Uses the Continental grip • Takes a short, compact backswing • Is ready to hit every ball

CHECKPOINT	BEGINNING LEVEL	INTERMEDIATE LEVEL	ADVANCED LEVEL
Swing			• Moves forward to make contact • Makes contact early • Usually hits with an open racket face • Keeps eyes level with the ball
Follow-Through			• Hits through the ball • Recovers for the next shot quickly

Error Detection and Correction for the Advanced Volley

Stand to the side of a player hitting volleys. Watch to see whether the weight is forward in anticipation of the shot before it is hit. Then notice the length of the backswing: If you can see the entire racket behind the player's body in preparation for the volley, the backswing is probably too long. Finally, watch for the point of contact: Make sure it is well in front of the body instead of even with or behind the player's position at the net.

ERROR

CORRECTION

ERROR	CORRECTION
1. Student changes grips.	1. Check the position of the wrist. Then have the player hit volleys while holding the off-hand (non-hitting hand) behind the back to avoid using it to help change grips. There is a tendency in many players to hit the first volley with the right grip, then to change it to a forehand on subsequent shots.

ERROR 🚫   **CORRECTION**

2. Student lets the ball drop.

2. Have the student get to the ball on the rise, not after it starts descending. If the ball is allowed to drop, the volleyer has to hit up on the ball, making the opponent's next shot easier. If the ball is hit sooner, while it is rising or at its peak, the volleyer can hit an offensive, power volley.

3. Student exhibits excessive backswing.

3. Tell your student not to draw the racket back any farther than the back foot. Stand behind the player and restrict the swing. In practice, make the player prepare for the volley by placing the racket on the net; then feed shots in which there is no time for a long backswing. Emphasize a short, firm punch at the ball, unless there is plenty of time for a bigger backswing.

ERROR	CORRECTION
4. Student has a loose grip.	4. At advanced levels, the ball comes with more pace. The student must hold on tighter, especially as the ball approaches. In quick exchanges, he or she must expect every shot to come back immediately. The volleyer should not be surprised by anything but should expect trouble and be ready for it.
5. Student waits on the ball.	5. Tell the student to get to the ball before it gets to him or her. Contact must be made in front of and to the side of where the player is standing. The ball must not be allowed to drop; it should be hit while it is rising. Watching the opponent's racket face helps the student anticipate where the ball is going.
6. Student uses a two-handed backhand.	6. Although there are successful players who use two hands from the baseline, very few have effective two-handed backhand volleys. The racket is hard to maneuver, and there is a tendency for the racket face to turn over so much that it forces the ball into the net. Early on, start teaching players to grip with one hand, with support from the opposite hand. Forearm and grip strength exercises will make the one-handed backhand volley more comfortable and effective.

Advanced Volley Drills

Note: The order of these drills is not necessarily from easy to difficult because the difficulty of each drill depends on how advanced the individual player is. The drills are presented so that you can select those that are appropriate to the student or group you are teaching.

1. *Hand-Behind-the-Back Volleys*
[Corresponds to *Tennis*, Step 12, Drill 9]

Group Management and Safety Tips

- Put four to six players on a court with extra players retrieving balls.
- This drill is presented first (and out of sequence with the participant's book) because of the importance of teaching the correct volley grip for advanced players. With beginners and intermediates, the emphasis is more on getting used to playing at the net comfortably than on advanced grip technique.

Equipment

- Balls, at least 3 per student pair

Instructions to Class

- "Use the Continental grip to practice volleys. Put the off hand in your pocket or behind your back. A practice partner at the baseline then feeds a total of 25 shots to your forehand and backhand sides. Do not change grips. Keep your wrist directly in line with the top, flat edge of the racket handle. After each shot, put your arm and the racket well out in front of your body, pointing toward the other player."

Student Option

- "Put a coin between your little finger and the racket handle. If the coin falls out, you've been caught trying to change grips."

Student Success Goal

- 25 consecutive volleys without a grip change

To Decrease Difficulty

- Reduce the distance between hitter (or tosser) and volleyer.
- Have feeder set up balls at a softer pace.
- Allow player to use the opposite hand for support on the backhand side.
- Reduce the Success Goal to 20 or 15 volleys.

To Increase Difficulty

- Increase the distance between hitter (or tosser) and volleyer.
- Have feeder set up shots with more pace.
- Increase the Success Goal by increments of 5.

2. Two-on-One Volleys
[Corresponds to *Tennis*, Step 12, Drill 1]

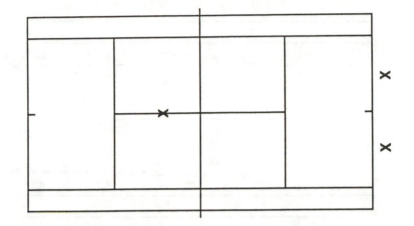

Group Management and Safety Tips
- Put three players on each court.
- Rotate players every 2 to 3 minutes.
- Continually check the grip of the volleyer.

Equipment
- Balls, 1 basket per court

Instructions to Class
- ''Take a position about 12 feet from the net on the center service line. You will volley against two partners who alternate putting shots in play to you from the baseline. Count as good every volley hit into the opposite singles court out of 20 attempts, then repeat the cycle. If you are volleying, recover quickly after every shot. If you are setting up shots, use good footwork and controlled groundstrokes to keep the ball in play.''

Student Option
- ''Request setups to your weaker side.''

Student Success Goal
- 15 of every 20-volley series going into the desired singles court

To Decrease Difficulty
- Have the volleyer move closer to the net, but then have feeders hit softer setups.
- Reduce the Success Goal to 10 of 20.

To Increase Difficulty
- Have feeders increase the pace of setups.
- Have feeders hit most shots to the weaker side of the volleyer.
- Increase the Success Goal by increments of 2.

3. Target Volleys
[Corresponds to *Tennis*, Step 12, Drill 2]

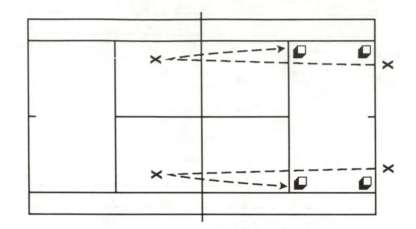

Group Management and Safety Tips
- Put four players on each court.
- Use waiting players to retrieve balls.
- Have students rotate positions every 2 to 3 minutes.

Equipment
- Balls, at least 3 per student pair
- Boxes or other targets, 1 per pair

Instructions to Class
- "Take a position about 10 to 12 feet from the net. Have your practice partner place a target in four sites: deep backhand corner, deep forehand corner, where the right service line meets the singles sideline, and where the left service line meets the singles sideline. Your partner will set you up with a variety of high, low, straight-ahead, wide, hard, and soft shots to volley. Count every volley that hits the target placed in the opposite singles court."

Student Option
- "Alternately hit forehand and backhand volleys without changing your grip."

Student Success Goal
- 5 out of 10 volleys hitting the target

To Decrease Difficulty
- Move target closer to the volleyer.
- Have feeder set up the volleyer with similar shots every time.
- Reduce the Success Goal to 2 of 5.

To Increase Difficulty
- Move the target to various spots on the court.
- Have feeder increase the pace of shots set up for the volleyer.
- Increase the Success Goal by increments of 2.

4. *Consecutive Partner Volley*
[Corresponds to *Tennis*, Step 12, Drill 3]

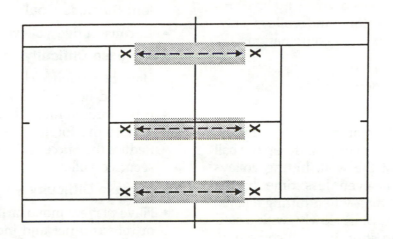

Group Management and Safety Tips

- Put up to eight players at the net hitting volleys (four against four) and use eight more players to retrieve while waiting their turns.

Equipment

- Balls, at least 3 per student pair

Instructions to Class

- "You and your partner stand about 15 feet from, and on opposite sides of, the net. Count the number of consecutive shots you hit to each other using only volleys. Do not try to win points; just keep the ball in play with medium-paced volleys until both of you are used to the routine. As soon as you hit, recover for the next shot. Work on taking pace off of the ball, when it is necessary for control, by slightly loosening your grip."

Student Option

- "Hit series of volleys using forehands only, then backhands only, then combinations."

Student Success Goal

- 15 consecutive volleys

To Decrease Difficulty

- Reduce the distance between players, who then hit softer shots.
- Have students practice the routine without a net.
- Reduce the Success Goal to 10.

To Increase Difficulty

- Increase the distance between players.
- Reduce the number of players to four on each court and have them hit crosscourt volleys instead of straight-ahead shots.
- Increase the Success Goal by increments of 5.

5. *Wall Volleys*
[Corresponds to *Tennis*, Step 12, Drill 10]

Group Management and Safety Tips

- Allow at least 15 feet between players to avoid accidental contact.
- Encourage controlled volleys. Have students start with forehand volleys only, then backhands, then combinations.

Equipment

- Balls, 2 per student

Instructions to Class

- ''Take a position approximately 15 feet from a rebound net or wall. Keep the ball in play against the wall, hitting volleys only. There is even less time hitting against a wall than when hitting against another player. Start slowly, with a soft, medium-paced shot that will come back to your forehand. Then try to pick up the pace as you get used to the rebound off the wall.''

Student Option

- ''Alternate hitting forehand and backhand volleys.''

Student Success Goal

- 12 consecutive volleys

To Decrease Difficulty

- Have player move closer to the wall or the rebound net and hit softer volleys.
- Have student hit so that shots come back only to the forehand side.
- Reduce the Success Goal to 6, 8, or 10 consecutive volleys.

To Increase Difficulty

- Have players move farther from the wall or rebound net and increase the pace.
- Increase the Success Goal by increments of 2.

6. *Team Consecutive Volleys*
[New drill]

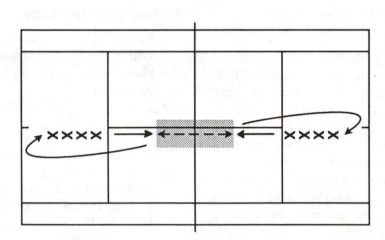

Group Management and Safety Tips

- Put 8 to 20 players on each court.
- Balance teams with combinations of strong and weak players.
- Have plenty of spare tennis balls ready to replace those hit out of reach.

Equipment

- Balls, 3 per court

Instructions to Class

- ''Divide into two teams of at least four players on each court and take a position in line starting at the service line. Keep the ball in play by hitting a volley, then move to the end of your line. Move in quickly when it is your turn to hit. As soon as you hit, move out of the way for the next player; don't wait to see what happens with your shot.''

Student Option

- ''Compete against a player on your team or challenge the other team for the most consecutive volleys.''

Student Success Goal

- 15 consecutive volleys between the two teams

To Decrease Difficulty

- Have players move closer to the net and reduce the pace of shots.
- Place one consistent volleyer alone on one side of the net to stabilize the drill, with all other players lining up across the net and taking turns hitting.
- Reduce the Success Goal to 10.

To Increase Difficulty

- Have each player hit two volleys before moving out.
- Have players move farther from the net and increase the pace of volleys.
- Increase the Success Goal by increments of 5.
- Make players move to another court with two misses.

7. Volley–Volley Up
[Corresponds to *Tennis*, Step 12, Drill 5]

Group Management and Safety Tips

- Put four players on each court.
- This drill will work only with advanced intermediate and advanced players.

Equipment

- Balls, 3 per student pair

Instructions to Class

- ''Take a position near the center of the service line between the singles sideline and the center service line. A partner stands in a similar location across the net. Put a ball into play and keep it in play with volleys. However, before each volley, you must stop the ball by bumping it up in the air to yourself; then you volley it across to your partner. Loosen your grip slightly to take speed off of the ball and tilt your racket face up just a bit to bump the ball into the air.''

Student Option

- ''Count the number of consecutive volleys hit.''

Student Success Goal

- 6 consecutive bump-ups and volleys

To Decrease Difficulty

- Have the partner just toss the ball to the volleyer rather than have two volleyers keep the ball in play.
- Have student try to hit softer volleys across the net so the partner has more time to react and control the ball.

To Increase Difficulty

- Increase the distance between volleyers.
- Have volleyers increase the pace of volleys.

8. Closing Volleys
[Corresponds to *Tennis*, Step 12, Drill 7]

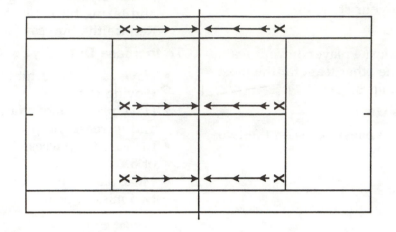

Group Management and Safety Tips

- Put eight players on each court: one on one, four pairs on each court.
- Put only six players on each court when they are less skilled.
- Let players begin by volleying without closing in until they get into a volleying rhythm.
- Use waiting players to retrieve balls.

Equipment

- Balls, 3 per student pair

Instructions to Class

- "Take a position at the service line in the center of the court. Put a ball into play to your partner at the opposite service line. With each controlled volley, move a half-step closer to the net. Do not overhit. Keep the ball under control, move in as you hit, and recover quickly for the next return. Keep your racket up so that you are looking directly over the top of its frame between shots."

Student Option

- "With each miss, either put another ball into play from where you missed or move back to the service line and start again."

Student Success Goal

- Move close enough to the net to touch it without missing a volley

To Decrease Difficulty

- Have volleyer advance to the net after every other hit.
- Have volleyer reduce the pace of volleys.
- Have volleyer direct shots to the same side (either backhand or forehand) each time so the partner can anticipate the next shot.

To Increase Difficulty

- Have volleyer take a full step forward after every volley.
- Have volleyer increase the pace of the volleys.

9. Three-on-One Volleys
[New drill]

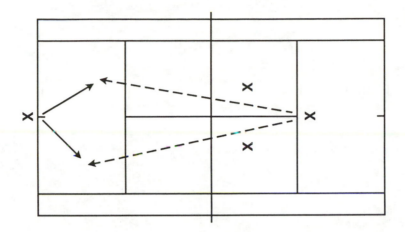

Group Management and Safety Tips

- Instruct the players at the net not to look back when they do not hit the ball; the third player on their side might hit them with a volley.
- The single player can use the opposite doubles court. The three volleyers can use only the opposite singles court.
- A fifth player can rotate in after 10 errors by the baseline player or after every 3 minutes.

Equipment

- Balls, 1 basket per court

Instructions to Class

- "Two players take positions side by side about 10 feet from the net, each in one of the service courts. A third player stands behind them at the center of the service line with a basket of balls. A fourth player stands at the center of the opposite baseline. The player at the service line puts balls into play to the baseline player, who hits groundstrokes back to the other three players, who practice controlled volleys. Volleyers should keep the ball in play rather than try to win points. Baseline players should hit and recover. Go for winners when you get the opportunity. Move to cover the space you leave open after wide shots. Rotate when I give the signal."

Student Option

- "The three on one side could compete against the baseline player by keeping score. The first player or team to win 10 points wins the game."

Student Success Goal

- One round without a volley error

To Decrease Difficulty

- Require the baseline player to hit controlled groundstrokes rather than attempt winners.
- The first shot of every series could be put into play so that the baseline player can hit a relatively easy forehand or backhand groundstroke.

To Increase Difficulty

- Allow the volleyers to go for winners.
- The ball could be put into play with more difficult shots.

10. Hot Seat Volleys
[New drill]

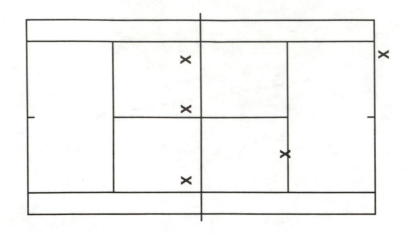

Group Management and Safety Tips

- Place five players on each court.
- Have the feeder keep the first shot low to protect the player in the hot seat.
- Have students play 10-point games, then rotate players.

Equipment

- Balls, 1 basket per court

Instructions to Class

- "Three players take volleying positions about 12 feet from the net. A fourth player sets up at the left (or right) side service line across the net, a position we'll call the 'hot seat.' A fifth player, on the fourth player's side, puts the ball into play to any of the first three players, who then hit volleys toward the player in the hot seat. Play the point out. If you are one of the three volleyers, hit forceful, winning volleys but don't try to deliberately hit the defending player on the opposite side. If you are in the hot seat, stay low between shots and keep your racket high and out in front of your body. Start out by just trying to get a few shots back. As you gain confidence, set a goal of winning points rather than just surviving."

Student Option

- "Move up or back one step from the service line, depending on your quickness and volleying ability."

Student Success Goal

- Survive the drill without getting hit.

To Decrease Difficulty

- Move the three volleyers farther from the net to increase the distance between them and the defender.
- Move the defender farther from the net to give him or her more time to react.
- Have the feeder set up the three volleyers with more difficult shots to protect the defender in the hot seat.
- Place only two volleyers against the player in the hot seat.

To Increase Difficulty

- Have the feeder set up the three volleyers with easier shots.
- Move the three volleyers closer to the net.

Step 13 Half-Volley

The half-volley is an emergency shot. Intermediate and advanced players will use the half-volley, but playing at that level does not mean that the shot automatically becomes part of a player's repertoire. In fact, the shot usually comes more with experience than with ability level. It requires racket control, confidence, quickness, and touch—attributes that are difficult to teach. All you can do as an instructor is to recognize the students who are ready to work on the shot and to give them practice hitting it.

STUDENT KEYS TO SUCCESS

- Hold the racket tightly
- Use the opponent's pace
- Bend and stay low
- Make early contact
- Stay with the shot

Half-Volley Rating

CHECKPOINT	BEGINNING LEVEL	INTERMEDIATE LEVEL	ADVANCED LEVEL
Preparation	• Not applicable	• Seldom anticipates the shot • May take excessive backswings	• Reacts quickly to shots hit at feet • Shortens the backswing
Swing		• Overswings • Has little control or feel for the shot	• Holds the racket tightly • Makes contact early • Uses the pace provided by the opponent
Follow-Through		• No different from other ground-strokes	• Complete swing to return softly hit shots • Blocks the ball and restricts the follow-through to return hard shots • Stays low on the shot

Error Detection and Correction for the Half-Volley

Watch for determination and hand-eye coordination on this shot. Quick, gutty players invent ways to stay in the point, even if they do not look good doing it. There is usually so little time to react that technique is second to results.

ERROR   **CORRECTION**

1. Student is out of position.	1. Tell your student to remember that the half-volley is an emergency shot. The student should stay out of the area of the court requiring such shots (between the service line and the baseline). The student should play from the baseline until there is an opportunity to get to the net, then move all the way in to a position in front of the service line. If a player gets caught between these two positions, he or she should be ready to hit lots of half-volleys.

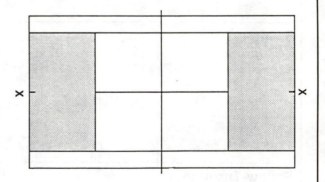

2. Student overreacts.

2. There is a tendency to fight power with power. Drive shots at your student, forcing returns with soft shots. Have him or her hold on tight against hard-hit shots, relaxing a little and providing some of the power against shots that do not come so hard.

ERROR	CORRECTION
3. Student gives up on the shot.	3. Many players just stick the racket down there and hope. However, the point is still in progress unless the ball is hit out or into the net. Have your student get down with the ball, hold tight, and make the ball go back. Returning half-volleys can be demoralizing to an opponent.

Half-Volley Drills

1. *Quick Hits*
[Corresponds to *Tennis*, Step 13, Drill 1]

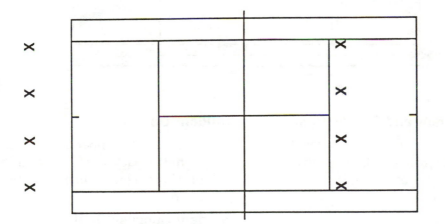

Group Management and Safety Tips
- Put up to eight players on each court.
- The drill will work with fewer balls, if 10 balls per student pair are not available.

Equipment
- Balls, at least 10 per student pair

Instructions to Class
- "Get a basket of balls and put them into play from a position just behind the service line by 'quick-hitting' them. Drop the ball on your forehand side, then, as soon as it bounces on the court, hit it into the opposite singles court. Your partner will retrieve 10 balls, then return them to you using the same technique."

Student Option
- "Count the total number of balls placed into the opposite singles half-court."

Student Success Goal
- 10 consecutive quick hits into the opposite singles court

To Decrease Difficulty

- Allow player to slow down the swing.
- Move player closer to the net.
- Reduce the Success Goal to 8 or 6.

To Increase Difficulty

- Move player closer to the net. Hitting quickly and controlling the ball is harder the closer to the net the player stands.
- Increase the Success Goal by increments of 2.

2. No-Man's-Land Rally
[Corresponds to *Tennis*, Step 13, Drill 2]

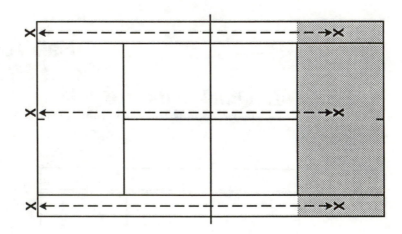

Group Management and Safety Tips

- Put up to six players on each court.
- Switch players from baseline to half-volley positions every 3 minutes.

Equipment

- Balls, 3 per student pair

Instructions to Class

- ''Instead of warming up with your partner in the normal baseline positions, move into the backcourt area (''no-man's-land''). Your partner will stay at the baseline until you switch positions. Keep the ball in play by hitting a combination of groundstrokes, volleys, and half-volleys. Hold your racket with a Continental grip to start the exchange. You may be able to change to conventional forehand and backhand grips when shots are returned to you with less pace.''

Student Option

- ''Count the number of half-volleys you hit from the backcourt area and the number of shots you return into the opposite court.''

Student Success Goal

- 10 consecutive returns from the backcourt area

To Decrease Difficulty

- Have student reduce the pace of shots.
- Reduce the Success Goal by to 8 or 6.

To Increase Difficulty

- Have student increase the pace of shots.
- Increase the Success Goal by increments of 2.

3. *Close-In Service Returns*
[Corresponds to *Tennis*, Step 13, Drill 3]

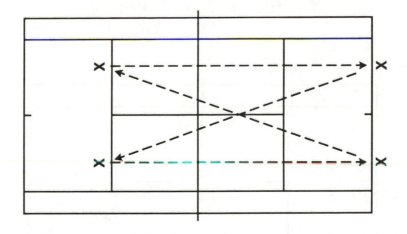

Group Management and Safety Tips

- Put four up to eight players on each court: six alternating serves from the left and the right sides, and two returning serves.
- Rotate the receivers to serving positions after 3 minutes.
- Do not have students play points out.
- Help players determine the correct receiving position, that is, the distance behind the service line from which they can effectively handle the serves and practice the half-volley.

Equipment

- Balls, 1 basket per court

Instructions to Class

- "Your partner will practice the serve while you practice returns from a position one step behind the service line. Bend your knees, lean forward, and take a short backswing as the serve approaches. The harder it comes, the less you have to swing. Just hold on tightly and block the ball back."

Student Option

- "Adjust your position according to your ability and the pace of the serve."

Student Success Goal

- 3 of 10 service returns into the singles court

To Decrease Difficulty

- Move the receiver farther away from the service line.
- Have the server serve at 3/4-speed.

To Increase Difficulty

- Move the server inside the baseline or move the receiver closer to the service line.
- Tell the servers to concentrate on hard, flat serves rather than spin serves.

4. Hot Seat Half-Volleys
[Corresponds to *Tennis*, Step 13, Drill 4]

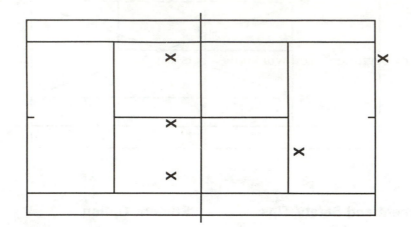

Group Management and Safety Tips

- Put five players on each court.
- Pair up physically to avoid large versus small players together.
- Have the feeder keep shots low to protect the person in the hot seat.

Equipment

- Balls, 1 basket per court

Instructions to Class

- "This is the same drill you might have practiced with the volley. You stand at the baseline, near a feeder with a basket of balls. Two [or three] players stand at the net opposite you. You take a position on either the right or left service line with the feeder behind you and to your side. The feeder sets up the volleyers, who hit shots directly at you. Dig out as many shots as you can with volleys and half-volleys. Stay low, hold your racket tightly, and play defense. Forget technique; just fight to get every shot back."

Student Option

- "Move back a few steps to have more time to react."

Student Success Goal

- 2 of 10 volleys or half-volleys

To Decrease Difficulty

- Move the player in the hot seat back a few steps.
- Move the opposing volleyers farther from the net.

To Increase Difficulty

- Move the opposing volleyers closer to the net.
- Have the feeder set up the volleyers with softer, higher shots.

Step 14 **Drop Shot**

The drop shot is another specialty shot used effectively by advanced players, attempted by intermediates and not used at all (or at least not on purpose) by beginners. You will know you are working with pretty good tennis players if they are using the drop shot. Like the half-volley, this shot comes as much from experience as it does from athletic ability. The percentage tennis player not only knows how to execute the shot—he or she knows *when* to use it. This time comes when an opponent has been driven deep behind the baseline or off to one side of the court, or when a hard, forcing shot is expected.

Teach your players to use the shot occasionally just so their opponents will be kept off balance enough to worry about it. The shot is especially effective against slow players, against players who are in poor physical condition, when the shot is hit against the wind, and when it is used on slow, rough-surfaced courts.

STUDENT KEYS TO SUCCESS

- Disguise the shot
- Swing high to low
- Open the racket face
- Finish the swing

Drop Shot Rating

CHECKPOINT	BEGINNING LEVEL	INTERMEDIATE LEVEL	ADVANCED LEVEL
Preparation	• Not applicable	• May telegraph the shot • May try the shot from the backcourt or baseline position	• Disguises the shot until the last second • Attempts the shot from the forecourt area
Swing		• Rotates the wrist excessively • May overhit or underhit • Swings level instead of high to low • Holds the racket too tightly	• Caresses the ball • Swings high to low • Hits with an open racket face • Does not hold the racket tightly
Follow-Through		• Stops swinging with contact	• Finishes the swing and recovers quickly

Error Detection and Correction for the Drop Shot

Inexperienced players telegraph the drop shot with earlier-than-usual preparation, different footwork, or unusual backswings. As you teach this shot, try to get students to prepare for it in the same way they prepare for groundstrokes or approach shots. Using an effective drop shot depends as much on surprise as it does technique. Ask players opposing the ones using drop shots whether they know when it is coming. If they can tell you or the hitters how the hitters let them know a drop shot is on the way, you can help the hitters disguise it more effectively.

ERROR

CORRECTION

1. Student misuses the shot.

1. Tell your student to hit the drop shot from the forecourt (shaded areas), when a slow opponent expects a deep drive, and when court and wind conditions are favorable. The student must be selective. Experimenting with the shot in a game or set comes only with a comfortable lead.

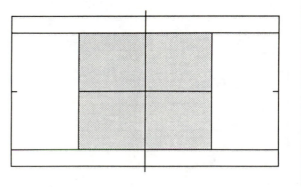

ERROR	CORRECTION
2. Swing is level.	2. The swing should be high to low with an open racket face. Have your student start the racket from a position slightly higher than normal. With the swing, the racket face should be tilted upward enough to give the ball backspin as it clears the net. The backspin will make the ball slow down and bounce lower after it hits the court, giving the opponent less time to get to the ball.
3. Grip is tight.	3. Have your student hold the racket more loosely than on groundstrokes. All of the fingers should be touching the handle, but not so tightly that there is not a good feel for the shot. The only way to get this feel is to practice as much as possible so as to recognize it and use it in drill and game situations.
4. Student uses too much wrist.	4. Some players try to curl the racket face around and under the ball by exaggerating the use of the wrist. Although the wrist may be used more on this shot than on others, many drop shots are missed, because the possibility of errors is greater with the added movement of the wrist. Have your student use the wrist to maneuver the racket face, but without overdoing it. The high-to-low swing with an open racket face is still the key to a good drop shot.
5. Student telegraphs the drop shot.	5. Question the player against whom the shot is tried. If the opponent can predict that it is coming, find out how. Then work with the player individually to eliminate the tip-off signs.

Drop Shot Drills

Note: Without using a specific drill format, pair the players and put them on opposite sides of the net, both close enough to touch it. Have them touch the ball in play as lightly as possible and still get it in over the net to their practice partners, keeping the ball in play as long as possible. Have your students constantly work on getting the ball lower and lower, so that it almost touches the net when it goes over. Do not emphasize success goals or scores; just get your students used to hitting with a feel for the shot. Drop shots do not have to be hit so delicately, but players at all levels need to practice touch shots like this one.

1. *Drop-and-Hit Drop Shots*
[Corresponds to *Tennis*, Step 14, Drill 1]

Group Management and Safety Tips

- Put up to eight players on each court, four hitting and four retrieving.
- Tell players that you want them to hit so softly that you cannot hear the ball when it touches the strings.

Equipment

- Balls, 3 per student pair

Instructions to Class

- "Stand at the service line. Drop the ball and hit a drop shot into the opposite service court so that it bounces twice before crossing the service line. Start with your racket slightly higher than on normal shots and swing in a high-to-low trajectory. Open the racket face a bit toward the sky as you hit. Think about trying to get the ball to land on top of the net as it descends. After 10 shots, let your practice partner hit drop shots into your court."

Student Option

- "Practice straight-ahead and crosscourt shots with a partner."

Student Success Goal

- 8 of 10 drop shots

To Decrease Difficulty

- Allow the ball to bounce only once in the opposite service court.
- Move players closer to the net.
- Reduce the Success Goal to 6 of 10 drop shots.

To Increase Difficulty

- Have player compete against a partner for more successful shots.
- Have student make the ball bounce three times within the opposite service court.
- Have student hit crosscourt drop shots instead of straight-ahead shots.

2. *Drop Shot Setups*
[Corresponds to *Tennis*, Step 14, Drill 2]

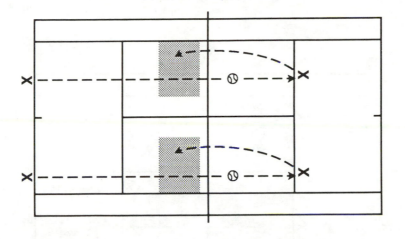

Group Management and Safety Tips

- Put four players on each court, each pair using only half of the singles court.
- Require feeders to hit medium- or slow-paced setups.

Equipment

- Balls, 3 per student pair

Instructions to Class

- ''Stand just behind the service line. Your partner drops and hits shots from the opposite baseline that bounce between you and the net. Return them with drop shots and play the point out. There is one catch, however: You do not have to return every shot with a drop shot. The idea is to disguise the shot so well that your baseline opponent does not know whether to expect a drop shot or a drive. After 10 points, switch positions with your partner.''

Student Option

- ''Compete by counting 1 point for every shot your partner places inside your service court and 1 point for each of your drop shots that bounces twice inside the opposite service court.''

Student Success Goal

- 5 of 10 drop shots

To Decrease Difficulty

- Have the partner toss balls from the opposite service line instead of hitting shots from the baseline.
- Do not have student play the point out.

To Increase Difficulty

- Have student hit some shots after the bounce and some as drop volleys, shots that are played as volleys but used as drop shots.
- Make the player hit drop shots on every setup, even though the opponent knows a drop shot will be hit, and play the point out.

3. *Short Game*
[Corresponds to *Tennis*, Step 14, Drill 4]

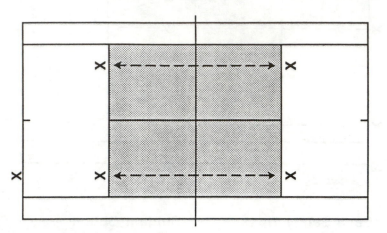

Group Management and Safety Tips

- Put up to four players on each court.
- If your class is small, let two players execute the drill using the entire forecourt area.

Equipment

- Balls, 3 per student pair

Instructions to Class

- ''Both practice opponents take positions just behind your respective service lines on either the right or left side. Play a game against your partner using only drop shots. Shots that are hit hard or bounce outside the service court are out of play. Use only half of the court, but include the alleys as within the boundaries. Remember to swing softly, putting backspin on the ball by turning the face of the racket upward at contact.''

Student Option

- ''If space permits, one player hits all down-the-line shots, and the other hits all crosscourt shots; then switch.''

Student Success Goal

- Play at least 3 games.

To Decrease Difficulty

- Do not have students keep score; they could play out points just for practice.

To Increase Difficulty

- Have students compete in drop shot tournaments or move to another court after lost games.
- Put two players on each court instead of four, to require more court coverage.

Step 15 Singles: Strategy and Formats for Competition

In this step, various forms of singles competition that can be used in a class or other group instruction setting are presented. These formats will have to be changed to fit the number of students you have and the number of courts and amount of time available to you and your students. Before these formats are described, here is a summary of the singles strategy suggestions given to students in *Tennis: Steps to Success* (Step 15), each item followed by comments to you.

GROUNDSTROKE TACTICS

- *Move to a position behind the center of the baseline between groundstrokes*. Inexperienced players tend to hit, stand, and watch to see where their shots land.

- *Hit most baseline groundstrokes crosscourt*. Prove to your players that by hitting crosscourt, they have more distance (therefore, space) with which to work, they have a lower net in the middle than on the sides, and they force the opponent to work harder to get to shots.

- *Hit most baseline groundstrokes deep into the backcourt*. If shots land deep, it is difficult for opponents to hit attacking shots. Draw lines parallel to and about 6 feet from the baseline; have players practice hitting groundstrokes between these two lines.

- *From the forecourt, hit shots at an angle to open up the court*. Players have a better view of the opposite court from a position at the net.

- *Use a shorter backswing against power players*. Get your players to practice shorter backswings by making them play inside the baseline during warm-up periods.

- *Use a shorter backswing on approach shots*. Emphasize that a full backswing added to the power generated by moving forward frequently causes players to overhit the ball.

- *Use a shorter backswing against fast serves*. Have students drive serves at receivers from a position well inside the baseline to practice this technique.

- *Keep the ball low when trying to pass opponents at the net*. Try to get your players to force the volleyer to hit up on the ball, rather than down on it for winners.

- *During baseline rallies, develop a pattern, then break it*. Suggest patterns to your players (like a quarterback calling plays in football), then have them practice those patterns.

- *A player weak on one side should leave space on the strong side to tempt the opponent to hit to that area*. Teach students to protect the court in areas of weakness and to force opponents to hit to strengths.

- *Stand near the baseline in the middle of the two extreme sides to which the ball can be served*. Stand behind the receiver to make sure he or she is covering the service court well.

- *Return short, weak serves parallel to the closest singles sideline*. Have three or four players take turns moving in to return serves down the line. They should move in, hit, and move out of the way for the next receiver. This simple drill will move fast, so several players can participate on the same court.

SERVING TACTICS

- *Stand near the center of the baseline to serve*. Position your players where they can get to a return anywhere on the court.

- *Do not waste energy trying to serve aces*. Work with your players to develop medium-paced serves that can be placed deep into the service court.

- *Develop two medium-paced serves, rather than one fast serve and one slow one*. Have students work on consistency rather than unpredictable power.

- *Serve to weaknesses or open parts of the service court*. Stand behind players before they serve and give instructions when necessary.

- *Be careful about serving to the receiver's forehand*. Explain that serving to the backhand is usually safer.

- *Serve wide to pull an opponent off the court*. Have servers and receivers walk through the possibilities to illustrate respective court positions following wide serves.

- *Serve deep to keep the opponent from attacking the serve*. Draw a line parallel to and about 4 feet from the service line; have players practice serving between the two lines.

- *Use spin on the serve for more control*. Show students how to lead the shot with the racket edge slightly forward instead of always hitting with a flat racket surface.

- *When serving, play more conservatively when the score is tied or when losing late in a game*. Have students play practice games in which the score begins at deuce, ad in, or ad out.

- *Experiment with a variety of serves during a match*. Use practice time to have a contest in which the player with the greatest variety of serves wins.

VOLLEY TACTICS

- *Stand near the center of the court and 10 to 15 feet from the net to hit most volleys*.

Place inexperienced players closer to the net until they are comfortable hitting volleys, then gradually move them back.

- *Place most volleys deep and into the open part of the court*. Stand behind players and help them determine where the open spots are located.

- *Use a crosscourt volley to return passing shots attempted down the line*. Show players that a crosscourt volley will usually put the ball into the space left open by the baseline player.

- *Use a down-the-line volley to return passing shots attempted crosscourt*. Logic related to that applied in the previous tip works here, also.

- *Move diagonally toward the net on volleys when there is time*. Demonstrate how much more power a player has when the body is moving forward than when it is moving parallel to the net.

- *Move closer to the net after a well-hit volley*. Tell players to be aggressive at the net and to move in for "the kill" after a good volley.

- *Use the first volley to set up for a winning second volley*. Inexperienced players frequently panic at the net and try to make every shot a winner.

- *When in doubt, volley deep to the opponent's weaker side*. Talk with players about where the weaker side is before points and games begin, then monitor the match to see whether they follow the plan.

- *Expect every shot to be returned*. Until players gain experience, they are often surprised when volleys come back faster than they left their own rackets.

LOB TACTICS

- *If mistakes are made on lobs, they should be made deep rather than short*. As with groundstrokes and serves, draw target lines on the court near the baseline for practicing deep lobs.

- *Use the lob more often when the opponent has to look into the sun*. Many times, players will not even be aware of the advantage the lobber has when the sun is a factor.

- *Hit most defensive lobs crosscourt*. Let your players practice both down-the-line and crosscourt lobs to illustrate the problems created for lobbers by lobs hit down the line.

- *Follow good offensive lobs to the net*. Use a three-shot sequence to practice this technique: The baseline player lobs over a player at the net; the net player retreats and returns the lob after the bounce; the lobber moves forward to the service line and tries to finish the point with a volley or a smash.

- *Lob occasionally just to make the opponent aware that the lob is a threat*. After a set ask players how many times they lobbed intentionally. If they cannot answer the question, it probably means they need to hit more lobs.

- *Lob high when in a defensive position*. Use a stopwatch to record "hang" times for lobs, then explain how higher lobs allow more time for recovery for the next shot.

- *Lob low when trying to win the point on that shot*. Have players practice lobbing over a player near the net whose arm and racket are stretched up as high as possible.

- *Hit most lobs to the backhand side of the opponent*. Have players practice this three-shot drill: (1) Lob to the backhand of a player at the net; (2) return the lob with a high backhand; and (3) move in to finish the point off a weak return.

SMASH TACTICS

- *Smash after the bounce if you can do it without losing your offensive position*. Let players practice smashes before and after the bounce to show them how much easier it is after the bounce from a forecourt position.

- *Do not let the ball bounce before a smash if you would lose the offensive position after the bounce*. Hit deep lobs to your students and let them practice smashes before and after the bounce to illustrate the problem.

- *Hit smashes flat from a position close to the net*. Let players hit smashes with and without spin to see the difference in the speed of the ball.

- *From the backcourt, hit smashes with spin*. From a deeper position in the backcourt, your students can try flat and spin smashes to get an idea of the control that spin smashes provide.

- *Change direction of second consecutive smashes*. Explain or demonstrate how much harder the retriever has to work against smashes directed to two parts of the court instead of just one.

- *When near the net, hit smashes at an angle*. Stand behind the player about to smash and help him or her determine where the open part of the opponent's court is.

- *From the backcourt, hit smashes deep and to a corner*. A simple two-shot, lob-smash drill to practice directing balls to corners will reinforce this strategy.

- *Do not try winning smashes from the baseline*. Play 5-point games in which the baseline player tries to win the point with an all-out smash from the baseline. Then play another 5-point game in which the same player hits controlled smashes to the opposite corners. Compare the results.

DROP SHOT TACTICS

- *Drop shots should be attempted only from the forecourt*. Have students play 5-point games in which they first try drop shots from the baseline, then from the forecourt. Compare game results.

- *Use drop shots against slow-moving players*. Discuss opponents and their abilities or weaknesses before matches to help your players formulate game plans.

- *Drop shots should not be tried when there is a strong wind at the player's back*. Stop play if a strong wind comes up during practice; explain the problem of the wind carrying the ball too far into the opponent's backcourt.

- *Drop shots should not be tried against fast players*. Most players will get this idea once they are beaten on a point following a drop shot.

Singles Formats for Competition
[New drills, except Drill 7]

1. Tringles

Tringles is a format for playing three separate singles matches at the same time on the same court. It is not two against one; it is a one against one game (A vs. B), another one against one (A vs. C), and another one against one (B vs. C). This game is more fun than having a doubles team play against a singles player, or the players having to rotate so that one has to sit out a game or set waiting for his or her turn. Here are the rules:

- Two players take turns playing singles points against a third player.
- These two players, on the same side of the net but alternating turns at playing points, always serve, beginning from the right as in regular play.
- The player receiving the serve plays alone, playing every point as long as he or she keeps on winning games.
- When a server wins a game, he or she changes places with the receiver just defeated, and their set score is noted. The other server must begin a new game

against the new receiver. The former receiver now becomes the second server.
- Play continues for as many games or sets as you, the instructor, allow.

Group Management and Safety Tips

- Use at least three balls per court, but four or five speed up play.
- Although grouping players is important, Tringles offers an opportunity to mix players of slightly different abilities and styles to compete against each other.
- If one player is significantly weaker than the other two, allow that player to receive serve and play alone first. This way, the weakest player is guaranteed at least one game playing every point.
- Keeping score can be difficult. Require the server to call out the score before each point.
- A set may take an entire class period, so keep track of the progress players make.
- Have the idle server pick up two balls and be ready to move in to serve immediately after the current point has been completed.

2. Winners Move Up

This form of competition requires that you have an even number of players and enough courts to accommodate all players. Singles or doubles can be played. Rules:

- Assign courts to all players at random.
- Keep score by points or games.
- Players or teams alternate serving 5 points each.
- At your command to stop, players who are ahead in total points or games won move up one court; those who are losing move down one court. Players winning on Court 1 stay there; those losing on the last court remain there.
- If a score is tied when play is stopped, determine a winner with a 1-point tiebreaker.
- Allow pairs of opponents at least 10 minutes of competition before you stop them.
- Players on Court 1 at the end of the period win the competition.

Group Management and Safety Tips

- Clearly establish the top and bottom (first and last) courts so players know which way to move after wins and losses.
- Points are scored consecutively, that is, 1, 2, 3, 4, 5, 6, and so on.
- Allow players to play approximately 10 points before changing courts. If scoring by games is kept, allow players to complete at least 3 games before changing.
- Although players are assigned courts randomly, at least some strong players should be placed on bottom courts at the beginning. They will then have to work up to the top instead of starting there.
- The first court change will confuse some students, so be ready to help with directions.

3. 4-Point Game

This is a simple game between two players, one at each baseline. Three to five other players wait behind each baseline for their turns to play. Play progresses rapidly, so players seldom have to wait more than 1 or 2 minutes. Waiting players can keep score or retrieve balls. Rules:

- The player at one baseline drops a ball and puts it into play against the opponent at the opposite baseline.
- Points are played out until one player wins 4 points.
- The player who wins gets to stay and play the next player, who has been waiting.
- The losing player moves to the end of the line on another court.

Group Management and Safety Tips

- Class size has to be reasonably small for this format. More than six players per court will make for too much standing in line.
- If the line on one court gets too long, allow one or more players at the end of that line to move to another court.
- If a player wins three consecutive games, consider moving another player into that position and requiring the winning player to move to another court.
- With advanced players, points may be started by serving instead of by dropping and hitting a ball into play.
- With all levels, the first shot put into play must be playable by the receiver. If not, the point must be restarted.

4. Ladder Tournaments

A ladder tournament is one in which the names of players are listed vertically and numbered consecutively from the top to the bottom of the list. The initial positions of the players may be determined by chance or may be ranked according to ability. Rules:

- A player may challenge a player who is ranked one or two positions higher.
- If the challenger wins, he or she changes places with the defeated player.
- Players cannot challenge the same person two consecutive times.
- Results are reported to you and then posted.
- Allow designated class periods for challenge matches or require that all challenge matches be played outside of class.

- Provide for nonladder competition when the number or availability of students does not allow for everyone to participate in the tournament.

Group Management and Safety Tips

- Good record keeping is essential. Require students to report match results immediately after play.
- Post results and standings on a bulletin board or wall so that every student in the class knows where he or she stands.
- Assign record-keeping responsibilities to students who do not dress out.
- If students are absent without prior notice, they may lose their position on the ladder.

5. Short-Court Games

This game is played using the service court lines as boundaries. Rules:

- A player starts a point by standing behind the service line on the right side, then dropping and softly putting a ball into play. The player alternates putting the ball into play from the left and the right sides.
- The point is played out by the players' controlling the ball and keeping it within the service court lines.
- No volleys are allowed.

- The first player to score 5 points wins the game.

Group Management and Safety Tips

- You will have to make judgment calls on whether or not balls hit hard are illegal volleys.
- Encourage students to settle their own arguments before asking for help.
- For a large class, each court may be used for two simultaneous games, one on each half of the singles court.

6. One-Serve Singles

This game can be used with any of the formats already described. The only difference is that the server or person putting the ball into play gets only one chance to do so. If the serve or shot is out of the boundary lines, that point is lost.

Group Management and Safety Tips

- Games will be completed quickly. Consider allowing court changes after every four games instead of after every two.
- Encourage students to use a normal service motion rather than a severely restricted one just to get the ball in, such as a punch serve.

7. Predetermined Points

In order to practice certain sequences of shots, two players agree to begin a point with a specific shot combination. Following are the situations described in *Tennis: Steps to Success*, Step 15:

Situation 1: Player A serves; player B returns the serve with a forehand or backhand groundstroke. The server keeps the serve deep and either to the receiver's weaker side or to the part of the service court left open. The receiver prepares for hard serves with short backswings, taking a slightly bigger backswing and providing some of the power on softly hit serves. [Corresponds to *Tennis*, Step 15, Drill 1]

Situation 2: Player A serves from either side; B returns with a lob. The lob should go deep to the backhand corner. If the server has to retreat to return the lob, the lobber moves into a position near the service line to hit a winning overhead or volley. [Corresponds to *Tennis*, Step 15, Drill 2]

Situation 3: Player A serves from either the right or left side; B returns with a short shot to the open side of the court. The server keeps his or her head up while hitting and moving

his or her weight through the shot. The receiver watches to see where the server stands to put the ball into play. The return goes to the side with more open space. If the shot is a forcing one, Player B moves forward to try to win with a volley from a position inside the service line. [Corresponds to *Tennis*, Step 15, Drill 3]

Situation 4: Player A stands behind the baseline, slightly to the right or left side, drops a ball, and hits down the line parallel to the closer singles sideline; B starts from a volleying position inside the service line and cuts the shot off at the net with a forehand or backhand volley. Player A keeps the ball low on passing shots. Player B remembers to move diagonally toward the net to cut off passing shots. [Corresponds to *Tennis*, Step 15, Drill 4]

Situation 5: Player A stands near the center of the baseline and hits a short shot to one side of the forecourt; B moves in and hits an approach shot down the line, parallel to the closest line. Player B should take a short backswing on approach shots; since the body weight is moving forward, care must be taken not to overhit the ball. A deep, hard approach shot should be followed to the net, making Player B ready to win the point with a crosscourt volley or an overhead smash. [Corresponds to *Tennis*, Step 15, Drill 5]

Situation 6: Player A stands near the center of the baseline and hits a shot that falls softly into the opponent's service court; B moves in and hits an approach shot; A returns with a lob. The lob should be hit crosscourt if Player A is driven deep into a corner. Player A should remember to lob deeply as well as crosscourt; if a mistake is made, it should be made by hitting the ball beyond the baseline rather than so shallow the opponent can win with a smash. Player B should be in a position near the net to finish the point if Player A makes a mistake on the lob. [Corresponds to *Tennis*, Step 15, Drill 6]

Situation 7: Player A starts from the baseline and hits a short shot; B moves in and hits an approach shot; A returns with a down-the-line groundstroke. Player B follows the approach shot by moving closer to the net and staying on a line behind the shot and slightly toward the center of the court. Player A doesn't try to pass with a crosscourt shot unless having gotten to the ball early. If attempting the down-the-line passing shot, Player A should immediately move to cover the part of the court left open when he or she moved to get the approach shot. [Corresponds to *Tennis*, Step 15, Drill 7]

Situation 8: Player A starts from a baseline position, drops a ball, and hits a forcing shot anywhere into the opposite backcourt; B returns with a lob deep, high, and preferably to the backhand side. A good lob should be followed by Player B's moving in toward the service line to prepare for the return. Following a weak, short lob, Player B should recover to the center of the baseline and try to anticipate which direction the smash will be hit. Player B should not wait until the ball is smashed to move but should take a chance in anticipating where it will go. [Corresponds to *Tennis*, Step 15, Drill 8]

Situation 9: Player A stands behind the baseline and hits a lob; Player B starts approximately 12 feet from the net in the center of the court and returns with a smash. B retreats quickly if the lob is deep. B plants the back foot and leans forward while hitting the smash, trying to keep the ball in front of his or her position. Player A tries to anticipate where the ball will be smashed and makes a move in that direction. A's moving will at least make Player B think about something besides hitting the ball. [Corresponds to *Tennis*, Step 15, Drill 9]

Situation 10: Players A and B start behind their respective baselines and hit consecutive lobs; the ball must bounce between the service line and the baseline. They keep the ball in play with a "moon ball" rally until someone makes a mistake by hitting a weak, short shot. They keep the ball high and deep by swinging from low to high. Each follows through in the direction he or she wants to hit. Each takes chances deep rather than hitting short shots that the opponent can attack. One finishes the point with any stroke that will win. [Corresponds to *Tennis*, Step 15, Drill 10]

Situation 11: Player A serves from either the right or the left side; B takes position where the baseline meets the singles sideline and returns with a short shot into either service court; A hits a forcing shot and advances to the net. Player A must try to anticipate whether B will then try a lob or a passing shot. Player A moves back quickly to set his or her feet for a smash, then moves forward quickly to win the point with a crisp volley to the open part of the court. [Corresponds to *Tennis*, Step 15, Drill 11]

Situation 12: Players A and B take positions at opposite service lines in the center of the court and hit consecutive volleys. The point begins after they have exchanged three consecutive volleys. The players hit low incoming shots back down the middle of the court; they hit high shots at angles for winners. They recover quickly after every shot with the racket out in front of the body and the arms forward. They stay on their toes and lean forward. They don't relax until the point has been won. [Corresponds to *Tennis*, Step 15, Drill 12]

Situation 13: Player A volleys from a position in the center of the court and approximately 12 feet from the net, while B, at the baseline, tries to pass A with groundstrokes. Player A puts the ball into play so that Player B can hit a groundstroke from the middle of the baseline. B keeps the ball low on attempted passing shots and aims for a spot between the singles sideline and Player A. A tries to cut off softly hit passing shots early by moving forward and laterally toward the net. Player A should remember that most down-the-line attempts should be volleyed crosscourt, and most crosscourt passing attempts should be volleyed down the line. [Corresponds to *Tennis*, Step 15, Drill 13]

Situation 14: Player A takes a position in the center of the court, about 12 feet from the net; B stands on or behind the baseline on the opposite side and lobs over A; and A retreats to retrieve the lob after the bounce. Player A moves back slightly to one side of the ball to return it with a forehand or backhand lob after catching up with it. B moves in behind the lob to a position on the service line. If A tries a passing shot, B moves in to cut it off with a volley. If A lobs short, B moves in closer for a winning smash. [Corresponds to *Tennis*, Step 15, Drill 14]

Situation 15: Player A starts in the forecourt area between the service line and the net and puts the ball into play with a drop shot; B moves forward to hit A's shot; if A can get a racket on B's shot, A lobs over B's head; B retreats to run the ball down. They play the point out with any appropriate shots. Player A watches B's racket face if he or she gets to the first drop shot. If B gets to the lob put up by A, B tries lobbing it back deep and high to the backcourt, giving him- or herself time to recover and get back into the point. [Corresponds to *Tennis*, Step 15, Drill 15]

8. Singles Attack

Two players start at opposite baselines, and one puts a ball into play. The players hit groundstrokes until one hits a shot that falls inside the service court area. The player on whose side the ball bounces short moves in and hits an approach shot, and the point is played out. The players return to their original positions to begin the next point. Each player should wait for the right opportunity to attack, making sure to get a shot on which he or she can move forward, hit deeply into a corner, and follow to the net. If such a shot does not present itself, the player should just keep the ball in play and wait for another chance.

Group Management and Safety Tips

- Watch to see that players attack on the right shots. Some will be so eager to get to the net that they will move in on shots that they hit from deep in their backcourts.
- Remind players to get depth on shots by hitting higher over the net, not just by hitting harder.
- When mistakes are made, talk to both players about what should have happened.
- After points have been completed, both players must return to positions on or behind the baseline to begin the next series of shots.

9. Tiebreakers

Pair off players and have them compete in 12-point tiebreakers (best two out of three). This format will help inexperienced players learn how to keep score and rotate using the tiebreaker rules, and to play under the pressure of close scores.

Group Management and Safety Tips

- After someone wins a tiebreaker, rotate the players to compete against different opponents.
- Stop play occasionally to ask about the score, about starting positions (left or right sides), and when players have changed ends of the court.
- Use waiting students to stand at the net and keep score.

10. Handicap Tournaments

Use a round-robin format, with players handicapped according to ability or experience. Handicaps may range from +3 points for the weakest players to −3 points for the best players. For example, in a 10-point game, if a player who is a +2 plays against one who is a −1, the match begins with the weaker player ahead 3–0. Handicaps can be adjusted after each round of competition, if necessary. Serves change when the combined scores of both players is a multiple of 5 points (for example, 3–2, 5–0, 6–4, or 7–3).

Group Management and Safety Tips

- Some students will not be comfortable with their handicaps. Explain that they can change their handicaps by their performance on the court.
- Experiment with each student settting his or her own handicap, but reserve the right to adjust handicaps.

11. Adjustable Game Scores

A second method of handicapping players allows for changes according to the score. If a player is ahead by one game, the opponent begins the next game ahead by 1 point (15–0 or 0–15). If a player is winning by two games, the opponent begins the next game ahead by 2 points (30–0 or 0–30). If a player leads by three or more games, the opponent starts the next game ahead by 3 points (40–0 or 0–40).

Group Management and Safety Tips

- Players start serving on the side indicated by the score, even if the score was established before the start of the game. For example, after the first game, one player will be ahead 1–0 and may be serving at 0–15 to start the second game. The first serve will thus be put into play from the left side.

Step 16 Doubles and Mixed Doubles: Strategy and Drills

Following is a summary of the doubles strategy suggestions presented to students in Step 16 of *Tennis: Steps to Success*, each item with comments directed toward teachers and coaches.

GROUNDSTROKE TACTICS

- *Receive serves from a point approximately where the baseline meets the singles sidelines*. Explain to students that since the server usually moves farther toward the sideline in doubles, the receiver's position must change to cover the greater angle of the serve.

- *Stand just inside the baseline against players with weak serves*. Most players have a habit of lining up in the same position regardless of how hard the server hits the ball. Help your players recognize the opposing servers against whom they can move in for a stronger return.

- *If the server stays on the baseline following the serve, return deep and crosscourt, then move in behind this return*. It is important that doubles players develop an aggressive attitude, and the service return is a good shot with which to practice aggressiveness.

- *Aim for the singles sideline when trying to pass the server's partner at the net*. Inexperienced players think they have to hit the lines to win points. Teach them to leave room for error.

- *Attempt to pass the net player occasionally, even if the point is lost*. Players have to understand that showing a variety of shots and strategies complicates the work of their opponents.

- *Shift to cover the open court when a partner is pulled out of position*. Use an image of the two doubles partners being connected by an elastic rope. When one moves, the other has to move, also.

- *Let the player with the forehand take most of the shots that come down the middle*. This should be taught very early and should become a habit that players fall into without even thinking.

- *From the baseline, most shots should be hit low and down the middle against opponents at the net*. Informal drills with one team at the net against another on the baseline are a good way to practice this strategy.

- *Do not rely on groundstrokes to win in doubles*. Keep telling your students to get to the net. It is simply easier to win points from this position—especially with a partner covering half of the court—than it is to hope for something nice to happen from the baseline.

SERVING TACTICS

- *Stand about halfway between the center mark and the doubles sideline to serve*. This position gives the server a better angle for the serve and puts him or her closer to the side to cover shots returned to the alley.

- *Hit most serves at 3/4-speed and deep to the backhand or an open area*. Very few players can consistently hit hard enough to overpower players with full-speed serves over the course of a long match.

- *Serve wide to the right-hander's backhand in the odd (left) court*. Tell the player at the net to cover the alley while the server covers the middle of the court. Few opponents can win with a crosscourt return following a wide serve to the backhand.

- *Serve wide to the left-hander's backhand in the even (right) court*. The same tactic applies to this situation as in the previous one.

- *Let the stronger server begin serving each set*. Don't let egos and feelings get in the way of good strategy.

- *Serve down the middle if your partner is good at poaching*. Serves down the middle usually result in returns down the middle, easy for a good volleyer to reach and put away.

- *Use more spin on serves to get time to move toward the net*. Players have to realize that while hard-hit serves may look good, they allow the server very little time to get into a volleying position.

VOLLEY TACTICS

- *The server's partner should stand about 8 to 12 feet from the net and two or three steps inside the singles sideline to begin a point*. Beginning and intermediate players tend to stand too close to the net and too close to the alley. Make them take up some court space.

- *When a serve is hit wide, the player at the net should shift slightly in that direction*. This is a very hard concept for inexperienced players to grasp; most of them want to dig in and protect their little space.

- *The server's partner should protect his or her side of the court, take weak shots down the middle, and be ready to smash any lobs that the server does not take*. Try to change the notion that the player at the net is just defending the alley.

- *In quick exchanges at the net, the last player to hit a volley should be ready to take the next shot if it comes back down the middle*. Teach students to play the point as if playing singles from the center service line to the alley.

- *The server's partner should tempt the receiver to try a passing shot down the alley*. Let players experiment in practice with how far out into the service court they can stand and still cover the alley.

- *Go for winners when poaching*. Don't let your players be so nice that they lose points.

- *Poach occasionally, even if points are lost*. Make your students be predictably unpredictable.

- *Poach more often when the server is serving well*. You may have to stop practice matches and remind players of this point. Some get into a habit of staying put regardless of what else is happening.

- *Poach less often if the server has a good volley*. Don't let net players take away the server's best shots.

- *Fake the poach at times*. This is a relatively sophisticated move, so don't expect many students to try it and don't let any of them overdo it.

- *During rallies, watch opponents' racket faces*. There is a tendency to watch eyes rather than rackets.

- *Play farther from the net against players who lob frequently*. Set up points in which the receiver tries to lob over a player who first plays close to the net, then begins points several steps back. Compare the results.

- *On the other hand, move closer to the net to start points against players who seldom lob*. Have your students take whatever advantage the other team is willing to give.

- *Retreat quickly and take a defensive position when the other team is about to hit a smash*. Teach players to protect themselves but also to stay in the point as long as possible.

- *The server's partner should stand farther from the net to start points when the serve is weak*. Extra time is needed for reacting to the service return.

- *Shift slightly with every shot to cover the open court*. Don't let volleyers become ''glued'' to the court. They should be moving slightly forward, backward, or to the side with almost every shot.

- *A strong volleyer should play farther from the net than usual when playing with a weaker partner*. He or she can cover more of the court than when closer to the net.

LOB TACTICS

- *Lob over the player closer to the net, then follow the lob to the net*. Have students play out this situation in practice until everyone knows where they should be and which shots should be hit.

- *Use the offensive lob against players who poach often*. Have your students practice this 3-shot drill: (1) serve, (2) poach or fake the poach, and (3) return the serve cross-court or down the line with a lob. Give points for guessing right instead of winning the exchange of shots.

- *When in doubt, lob deep and down the center of the court*. Help your players stay in the point even when there is uncertainty about what to do.

SMASH TACTICS

- *Smash the first lob to the outside part of the opponent's court*. This opens up the court by separating the two opponents, giving plenty of space for the next smash to get through for a winner.

- *Smash down the middle if it is open*. This shot can create confusion for the opponents about who should return it and may open up one of the sides for the next shot.

- *The partner with the stronger smash should take overheads down the middle of the court*. There is plenty of time to get set, so teach teams to use their strengths without one player dominating.

- *Hit smashes toward players in weak positions*. Don't let your players hit to hurt, but they should hit to win.

Doubles Drills

Note: Most of the forms of singles competition described in Step 15 of this book can be used in doubles. In this section, drills and activities specifically designed for doubles are presented.

1. *Doubles Attack*
[New drill]

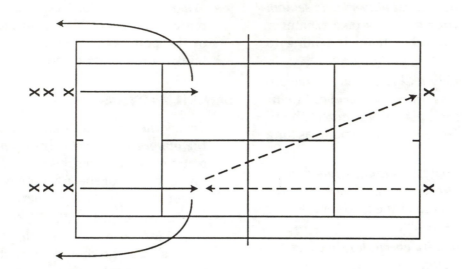

Group Management and Safety Tips

- Keep the teams rotating so that every team gets to play at least 10 points on the side by itself.
- Place three to five teams waiting in line behind the baseline. This drill moves very quickly; waiting for a turn never lasts for more than a few seconds. This drill works best with three or four doubles teams playing the attacking role.

Equipment

- Balls, 1 basket per court

Instructions to Class

- ''Two players stand at the baseline for each of two teams. One of the players puts a ball into play that lands softly in the opposite forecourt area. The opposing pair moves forward together, attacks the short ball, and plays the point out from the net position. When this point is over, the team that attacked moves out to the sides of the court for the next team, which had been waiting at the fence, to play its point. Attackers should wait for the right setup to attack. If the first shot does not land softly in your forecourt, return it and wait for a shot you like better.''

Student Option

- Not applicable

Student Success Goal

- Win at least half the points played.

To Decrease Difficulty

- Have the first hitters set up the first shot as softly as possible.

To Increase Difficulty

- Rotate out the team playing by itself if it loses two consecutive points.
- Place the strongest two doubles players on the side by themselves, setting others up with hard first shots. This will make the drill harder for the attacking teams.

2. Hit-and-Move Doubles
[New drill]

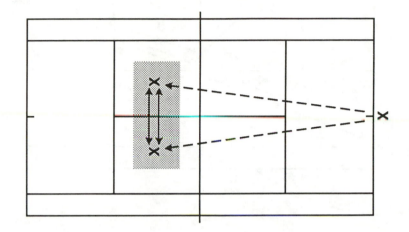

Group Management and Safety Tips

- Put three players on each court, one feeding and two volleying.
- Rotate volleyers every 30 seconds or after 10 consecutive volleys.
- This is a demanding drill, so it is best to have several student pairs per court waiting their turns to volley.

Equipment

- Balls, 1 basket per court

Instructions to Class

- ''Take a position with your partner approximately in the middle of the two respective service boxes. A feeder will put balls into play from the opposite baseline. You and your partner volley each ball back and quickly switch positions, crossing the center service line after each volley. This is a movement and conditioning drill as much as a technique drill. Learn to hit and move in coordination with your partner. Knowing which shots can and should be hit by which partner will make you a better doubles team. If your team hits 10 consecutive shots, rotate out and let another team take your place.''

Student Option

- Not applicable

Student Success Goal

- 10 consecutive volleys

To Decrease Difficulty

- Have feeder send slower paced balls.
- Position the volleyers closer to each other to begin the drill.

To Increase Difficulty

- Increase the Success Goal by increments of 2 or the time period allowed by 10-second increments.
- Have the feeder increase the pace of the balls.

3. Approach and Poach
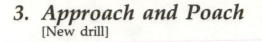
[New drill]

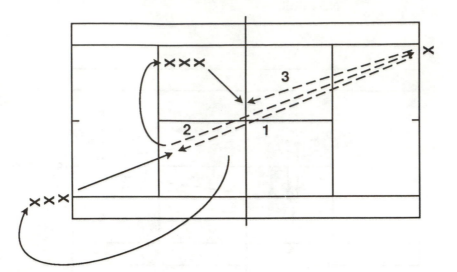

Group Management and Safety Tips

- Put up to eight players on each court.
- The drill will work only with a skilled feeder.
- Stop play when errors in technique or strategy occur; explain to the entire group what should have happened.

Equipment

- Balls, 1 basket per court

Instructions to Class

- ''Form two lines, one in the right-side serving position and the other in the server's partner position at the net. A feeder will stand on the opposite baseline in the right singles court corner and put the ball into play crosscourt and short to the first baseline player. This baseline player returns deep and crosscourt, then moves to the end of the line at the net. The feeder plays the shot and sets up the first player at the net for a poach at a point approximately in the middle of the net. After the poach, the net player moves out and to the end of the line at the baseline. If the feeder does not play the first crosscourt shot, a second ball is put into play for the poacher. If you are starting on the baseline, move forward, get set, then hit your groundstroke approach deep into the opposite corner. If you are at the net, move diagonally toward the net to cut off the ball with a volley, then get out of the way for the next series of shots.''

Student Option

- Not applicable

Student Success Goal

- 6 consecutive groundstrokes and poaches

To Decrease Difficulty

- The feeder could set up both players with softer shots.
- Alert players when it will be their turn to hit until they get into the rhythm of the drill.
- Reduce the Success Goal to 4.

To Increase Difficulty

- Increase the Success Goal by increments of 2.
- Conduct the same drill to the opposite side of the court, so that players have to approach and poach with backhand strokes.
- Have the feeder increase the pace of shots to both positions.

4. Defend the Net
[New drill]

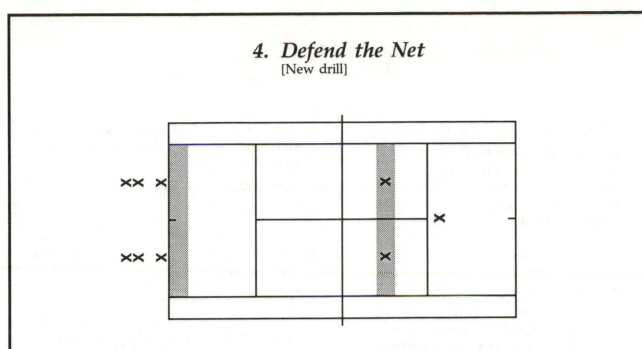

Group Management and Safety Tips
- Put five players on each court, with two to six more waiting to hit.
- Rotate the players at the net out if they win three consecutive 4-point games.

Equipment
- Balls, 1 basket per court

Instructions to Class
- "Two players take a position about 12 feet from the net, one in each service court, against two opponents at the baseline. A feeder will put balls into play from behind the first two players (volleyers), and the point is played out. The first team to score 4 points wins the game. The winning team gets to play at the net. Waiting teams move into the baseline position at the end of each game. Volleyers, get your weight on your toes and carry your rackets forward in anticipation of each shot. Baseline players, unless the volleyers get out of position, hit most of your shots low and down the middle of the court. Move in together to attack any short shots hit by the volleyers."

Student Option
- Not applicable

Student Success Goal
- Win at least one game.

To Decrease Difficulty
- Allow only controlled shots instead of attempts at winners.
- Make baseline players stay at their positions even if the volleyers hit weak or short shots, to make shots easier for the players at the net.

To Increase Difficulty
- Have the feeder set up the first shot deep or to the weak side of one of the baseline players.
- Make a rule that the ball must be kept in play for at least four shots before a point can be won.

5. Make My Day

[New drill]

Group Management and Safety Tips

- Put four players on each court.
- Rotate teams between courts for variety.
- Have teams play five games before rotating.
- Do not allow players to request smashes from distances too close to opponents.

Equipment

- Balls, 3 per court

Instructions to Class

- ''Ask the opposing team which shot they would like to have in order to 'make their day.' Allow that team to get into position to hit this shot and start the point where they want your team to begin, then set them up with their favorite shot and play the point out. If you are defending against a favorite shot, set a goal of winning at least 1 point out of every 5 you play. If your team is being set up, try for a perfect 5-for-5 winners.''

Student Option

- Not applicable

Student Success Goal

- 5 out of 5 points in which your team is set up for winners

To Decrease Difficulty

- Allow only favorite *baseline* setups, to make the drill easier for the defenders.

To Increase Difficulty

- Allow favorite shots to be hit from positions near the net, to make the drill harder for the defenders.

6. Situation Doubles

[New drill]

Instructions to Class

- ''Go to an assigned court and play the doubles situations described below 10 times each, then rotate positions on the court or play the next situation described by me. Play the point out after hitting the required shots.''
  - Serve, return serve to the player at the net.
  - Serve, lob over the player at the net.
  - Serve, return short and crosscourt.
  - Serve, return deep and crosscourt.
  - Serve and rush the net to volley the return of serve.
  - Serve, receiver returns deep and rushes the net.
  - Serve, return to the server's partner, volley to the receiver's partner.
  - Serve, return down the middle, server's partner poaches.
  - Serving team starts the point using the Australian formation: The server's partner lines up at the net in the same half of the doubles court as the server.
  - Serving team uses signals to indicate whether server's partner stays or poaches, and to indicate whether a serve will go to the inside or the outside.

Step 17 Adjusting to Opponents and Conditions

In *Tennis: Steps to Success* and in this book, Steps 15 and 16 give suggestions for using strokes in singles and doubles, respectively. Step 17 in the participant's book has information for playing different kinds of opponents in a variety of playing conditions. With that background, a few players who began the course as beginners, as well as most intermediates and any advanced players in the class, should be able to begin developing game plans. Following are questions that may be used for written assignments, as test items, or as classroom discussion topics.

The different strategies in singles and doubles dictate a difference in emphasis on certain strokes. What are the strokes, and how is the emphasis different?
- In singles, greater emphasis is on forehand and backhand groundstroke consistency from the baseline.
- Other strokes are important, but groundstrokes are the foundation for a winning singles game plan.
- In doubles, getting to the net and winning points from the forecourt are the keys to success. To do that, doubles players must have good serves, strong volleys, and smashes that can win points.
- Trying to win points in doubles with long groundstroke exchanges is not good strategy.

Develop a game plan for playing on a fast court against a right-handed big hitter.
- Play deeper on service returns.
- Chip the return to the opponent's feet when, as server, he or she follows the serve to the net.
- Do not get into a slugging match with a power player.
- Do not get discouraged if the big hitter makes you look bad on some points.

- Keep the ball as deep as possible and to the backhand corner.
- Serve to the inside corner of the service court from the right side and to the outside corner from the left side.

Develop a game plan for playing on a slow court against a left-handed retriever.
- Use a spin serve to the outside corner of the service court from the right side.
- Make the opponent come to the net as often as possible.
- Change the pace of groundstrokes; mix power shots with well-placed forehands and backhands from the baseline.
- Be patient; don't try to end the match too early. Work for it.

What are the advantages and the disadvantages of serving to the various target areas in singles and doubles?
- Serving wide to a right-hander's forehand in the deuce court forces the receiver wide but allows him or her to return with a forehand.
- Serving down the middle against a right-hander from the deuce court forces the receiver to return with a backhand, usually causing the return to come back down the middle of the court or off to the right side (as the server faces the net).
- Serving straight at players with big backswings reduces the amount of time they have to prepare for the return.
- Serving wide to a right-hander in the left court forces the receiver wide for the return and forces him or her to return with a backhand.
- Serving down the middle against a right-hander usually results in a down-the-middle return but allows the player to return with a forehand.

- Serving to the outside corner of the left service court against a left-hander is dangerous because it allows him or her to return with a forehand.

What do you consider the most important points in a game? How would you play those points differently from less important points?

- Many experts believe that the fourth point of a game, when the score is 30–15 or 15–30, is the most important point. If the player leading the game goes ahead at 40–15 or 15–40, he or she usually wins that game. If the score gets back to 30–30, it's anybody's game.
- Don't take chances on important points. Play aggressively, within your limits, taking advantage of your best shots and the opponent's weakest shots.

Give some guidelines for hitting approach shots in singles.

- Wait for shots that hit short in your forecourt.
- Don't try for winners on approach shots.
- Hit most approach shots down the line.
- Hit approach shots deep into the opponent's backcourt.
- Follow good approach shots to the net to be in a position to win the point with a volley or a smash.

Give some guidelines for returning serves in singles and doubles.

- If the server stays in the backcourt following the serve, return deep and crosscourt in doubles or deep to either corner in singles.
- If the server comes to the net following the serve, chip or block the return back to the server's feet.
- Do not try to win points on service returns.

How would you adjust your strategy if you were playing with a partner much stronger than you?

- Let the stronger player begin serving each set.
- Let the stronger player take shots that are returned down the middle of the court.

- Play closer to the net than normal when your partner serves.
- Do not poach often when your partner serves. Let him or her take the first return after a serve if the ball goes to that side.

What are the factors that should be considered in your deciding where to stand to begin a point as the receiver's partner?

- Start on the service line, halfway between the singles sideline and the center service line if your partner is returning serves well or if the server does not have a particularly strong serve.
- Start from the baseline if your partner is having trouble returning serves or if the server has a good serve.
- Start from the service line position on slow courts, because the pace of the serve will be slower on a rough surface.
- Start from the baseline position on fast courts, because the ball slides, bounces low, and is difficult for the receiver to return.

How can you use a strong wind to your advantage in singles?

- Get to the net more often because a wind at your back will give you more power and will send normal shots deeper into the backcourt.
- Play more aggressively against the wind. Take chances. The wind will help keep your shots inside the baseline.
- Stand inside the baseline to return serves when the wind will slow your opponent's serves.
- If you have a choice, start the match against the wind so you will be able to play the second and third games with the wind at your back.

How can you minimize the playing problems presented by extremely hot weather?

- Drink water before and during the match.
- Wear a hat.
- Alternate rackets every two or three games to keep the grips dry.
- Wear light-colored, loose-fitting clothes.

- Carry the racket in the nonhitting hand between points.
- Avoid unnecessary movement between points and games.
- Take a full 90-second break on odd-game changeovers.

How can physical capabilities and limitations affect a person's style of play?

- Physically strong players can use their power effectively on almost every shot.
- Players with good cardiopulmonary endurance do well in long matches.
- Players with good hand-eye coordination may play well at the net.
- Tall players make it difficult for opponents to lob over or pass when they are at the net.
- Shorter players may have an advantage of bending down on low shots and may be able to change directions more easily than taller players.
- Smaller players have difficulty covering drop shots.
- Players who are overweight have problems covering the court.

Give 10 examples of how the use of percentage tennis by your opponent can help you anticipate his or her shots.

- Expect most groundstrokes to be hit deep, high over the net, and crosscourt.
- Expect second serves to be hit with less pace and more spin.
- If you have a big backswing, expect serves to be hit directly at your body.
- Expect short, weak serves to be returned deep to a corner.
- If you attempt a down-the-line passing shot, expect a crosscourt volley.
- If you attempt a crosscourt passing shot, expect a down-the-line volley.
- If your opponent lobs over your head and you retreat to play the shot after the bounce, expect your opponent to follow the lob to the net.
- Expect most approach shots to be hit down the line.
- Expect two consecutive smashes to be hit in different directions.
- Expect the doubles net player to poach on strong serves down the middle of the court.

List the characteristics in a doubles partner that would complement your style of play.

- If you are right-handed, play with a left-hander.
- If you are a power player, play with someone who is consistent.
- If you are an emotional player, find a partner who is more even-tempered.
- If your strength is groundstrokes, get a partner with strong serves, volleys, and smashes.
- Play with someone you like and can get along with on and off the court.

Develop a game as if you were competing against yourself. How would you exploit the weaknesses in your own game?

Step 18   Concentration

Successful instructors teach concentration at two levels when working with tennis players. At the beginning level, players must learn how to focus on the ball and how to get all of the body parts working together to produce effective strokes. At a more advanced level, players give very little thought to the mechanics of stroke production, but must learn how to block out external distractions such as people, noise, or bad weather. While the beginner must concentrate just to get the ball over the net, the advanced player thinks about how to play points, games, sets, and matches. In both cases, the player's ultimate objective is to keep his or her mind from wandering while trying to master a sport that can be as difficult as it is fun. The good news is that concentration is not necessarily related to advanced strokes. Some beginners are able to focus totally on the task at hand, while some advanced players never develop concentration skills that match their playing ability. Although you—the teacher—cannot force a player to concentrate, you can help that player develop concentration skills.

STUDENT KEYS TO SUCCESS

- Focus attention on the ball
- Detach mind from distractions
- Plan points
- Control intensity
- Use little or no self-talk

Error Detection and Correction for Concentration

The task of evaluating the concentration levels of individual players while you teach a large class requires much concentration itself. You may have to watch a player for several minutes in order to observe lapses in concentration. While you do that, the rest of the class gets less of your attention than it should. However, there are some bad habits that can be observed and corrected by an alert instructor. Here are some of them:

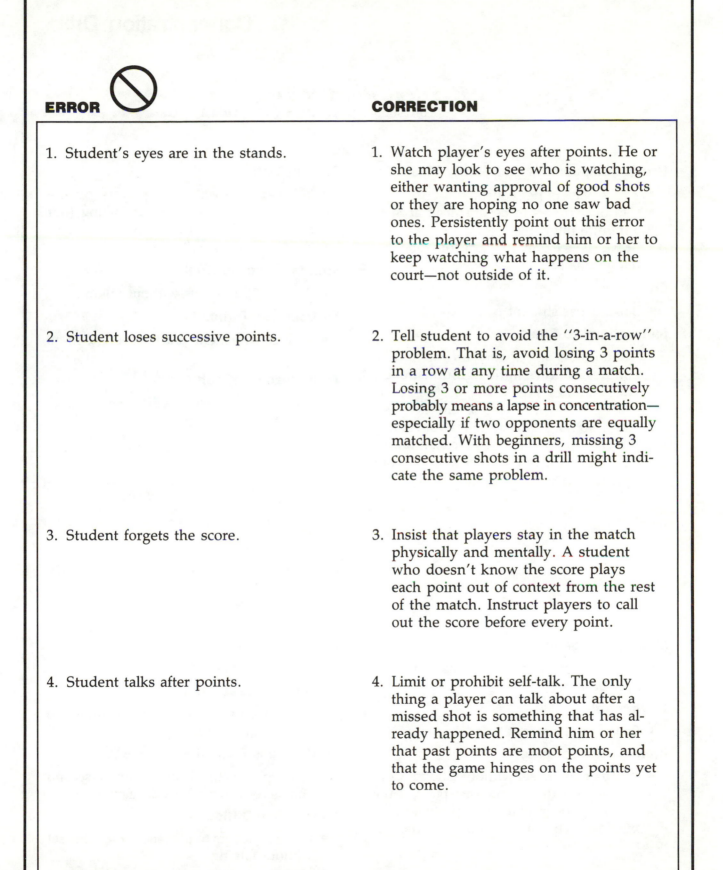

ERROR

CORRECTION

1. Student's eyes are in the stands.

1. Watch player's eyes after points. He or she may look to see who is watching, either wanting approval of good shots or they are hoping no one saw bad ones. Persistently point out this error to the player and remind him or her to keep watching what happens on the court—not outside of it.

2. Student loses successive points.

2. Tell student to avoid the "3-in-a-row" problem. That is, avoid losing 3 points in a row at any time during a match. Losing 3 or more points consecutively probably means a lapse in concentration—especially if two opponents are equally matched. With beginners, missing 3 consecutive shots in a drill might indicate the same problem.

3. Student forgets the score.

3. Insist that players stay in the match physically and mentally. A student who doesn't know the score plays each point out of context from the rest of the match. Instruct players to call out the score before every point.

4. Student talks after points.

4. Limit or prohibit self-talk. The only thing a player can talk about after a missed shot is something that has already happened. Remind him or her that past points are moot points, and that the game hinges on the points yet to come.

Concentration Drills

1. *Silent Practice Drill*
[Corresponds to *Tennis*, Step 18, Drill 1]

Group Management and Safety Tips

- 2 to 4 players per court
- Call out strokes to be practiced at 3- to 5-minute intervals.
- Break silence only to warn someone of a dangerous hit.

Equipment

- Balls, 3 per student pair

Instructions to Class

- ''Without saying a word for the next 15 minutes, practice hitting groundstrokes, volleys, and serves with a partner. I will instruct you which types of strokes to use. Allow nothing to distract you from hitting the ball. Keep your eyes focused on the ball, the court, and the racket face of your practice partner.''

Student Option

- ''If there are only two players on the court, play points without talking (not even to call out the score) instead of practicing strokes.''

Student Success Goal

- Practice 15 minutes without talking.

To Decrease Difficulty

- Reduce the silent practice period to 10 minutes.

To Increase Difficulty

- Increase the silent practice period to 20 minutes.

2. *Silent Set Drill*
[Corresponds to *Tennis*, Step 18, Drill 2]

Group Management and Safety Tips

- 2 to 4 players per court (singles or doubles may be played)

Equipment

- Balls, 3 per student pair

Instructions to Class

- ''Play an entire set without talking. Concentrate on the continuous path of the ball, on good stroking technique, and on playing each point as if it were the last point in the match.''

Student Option

- Not applicable

Student Success Goal

- Complete a set without talking, except to call out the score.

To Decrease Difficulty

- Allow players to talk during the 90-second change of court after odd games.

To Increase Difficulty

- Instruct players to play more than one set without talking.
- Do not allow players to call out the score.

3. Jam Box Tennis Drill

[Corresponds to *Tennis*, Step 18, Drill 3]

Group Management and Safety Tips

- Do not use this drill if it will distract others on the court who are not part of your class.

Equipment

- 1 radio or tape deck

Instructions to Class

- "During today's class, I will play a radio at a distracting volume. Retain your concentration. Do not let the noise bother you. Keep doing the drills or playing the points as though everything were normal."

Student Option

- Not applicable

Student Success Goal

- Participate in class activities while blocking out loud noises.

To Decrease Difficulty

- Decrease the volume.

To Increase Difficulty

- Increase the volume.

4. Take-Your-Best-Shot Drill

[Corresponds to *Tennis*, Step 18, Drill 4]

Group Management and Safety Tips

- 2 to 4 players per court (singles or doubles)
- Use the drill to provide practice of specific put-away situations on all courts.

Equipment

- Balls, 3 per student pair

Instructions to Class

- "Play 10 points in which you set up a practice partner with his or her favorite, can't-miss, finish-the-point shots. Then play the point out. Keep score, then reverse roles. Concentrate hard, intending to finish the point or at least to stay in the point regardless of the circumstances."

Student Option

- "Keep a running score to determine a winner after every 20-point series."

Student Success Goals

- 2 of 10 points won when setting up shots
- 8 of 10 points won when set up for winning shots

To Decrease Difficulty

- Require the put-away shots to be hit from the backcourt to make the drill easier for the defender.
- Allow the put-away shots to be hit from the forecourt to make the drill easier for the player being set up.

To Increase Difficulty

- Reduce the winning-shot target area to one side of the singles court to increase difficulty for the player being set up.
- Increase the singles target area to the doubles boundaries to increase difficulty for the defender.

5. 0–40 Game
[Corresponds to *Tennis*, Step 18, Drill 5]

Group Management and Safety Tips

- 2 to 4 players per court (singles or doubles)

Equipment

- Balls, 3 per student pair

Instructions to Class

- "Play a set in which every game is started with the score 40–0 or 0–40 against you. Try to win at least one game by maintaining your poise and concentration and by overcoming difficult situations."

Student Option

- Not applicable

Student Success Goal

- 1 game won in the set

To Decrease Difficulty

- Allow the player with the scoring disadvantage to choose whether to serve or receive.
- Begin games with a score of 15–40 or 40–15.

To Increase Difficulty

- Allow the player or team with the scoring advantage to choose whether to serve or receive.

6. Obstacle Course Tennis
[Corresponds to *Tennis*, Step 18, Drill 6]

Group Management and Safety Tips

- 2 to 4 players per court
- Select obstacles that are lightweight and movable.

Equipment

- 4 boxes, towels, racket covers, or other obstacles per court

Instructions to Class

- "Play a set with four harmless obstacles such as towels or racket covers placed on your side of the court. Put one in each service court and two in the backcourt area. Hit your strokes without being distracted by the obstacles on the court. If your opponent hits an obstacle, you lose the point."

Student Option

- Not applicable

Student Success Goal

- 1 set completed with obstacles on the court

To Decrease Difficulty

- Use smaller or fewer obstacles per court.

To Increase Difficulty

- Increase the size or number of obstacles.

7. Plan-a-Point Drill
[Corresponds to *Tennis*, Step 18, Drill 7]

Group Management and Safety Tips

- 2 to 4 players per court (singles or doubles)
- Move from court to court, asking students what their plans are before points begin.

Equipment

- Balls, 3 per student pair

Instructions to Class

- "Plan a point in your mind, then try to play it out against an opponent in a practice set. For example, you might plan first where to serve, then where to return, how much pace to put on the first ground-stroke, and finally, how to finish the point with a volley or a smash. Think through the entire sequence of shots in a point, then carry out your plan at least once a game."

Student Option

- "Allow one player to 'cooperate' by returning balls so his or her opponent can carry out the plan."

Student Success Goal

- 1 planned point executed in each game played

To Decrease Difficulty

- Allow players to plan and execute 1 or 2 shots during a point rather than planning the entire point.

To Increase Difficulty

- Allow points only when the plan is executed, even if the point is won by deviating from the plan.

8. Goal-Setting Drill
[Corresponds to *Tennis*, Step 18, Drill 8]

Group Management and Safety Tips

- 2 to 4 players per court (singles or doubles)
- Check to see that students are setting realistic goals.

Equipment

- Balls, 3 per student pair

Instructions to Class

- "During a practice set, establish goals to improve your concentration. Give yourself one point every time a goal is reached. You might set goals of holding the serve 3 times, committing no double faults, winning a game on the first game point, winning the first point of at least 4 games, returning 1 shot no one would expect you to return, breaking your opponent's serve once in a set, or returning every serve."

Student Option

- "Set goals to improve weak areas such as second serves or backhands."

Student Success Goal

- 2 goals reached in one set

To Decrease Difficulty

- Reduce the number of goals per set to one.

To Increase Difficulty

- Increase the number of goals to be reached during a set.

Step 19 Learning by Watching

In Step 19 of *Tennis: Steps to Success*, students are given three forms to complete—Postmatch Scouting Form, Error Chart, and Winning Shot Chart. If time permits, ask the students to complete these forms and turn them in to you. Then either schedule time to discuss the results of the matches observed with each student or devote one class period to a group discussion of the results.

The *Postmatch Scouting Form* gives a player the opportunity to make notes on a match after it is completed. The notes can then be used to analyze a match or to prepare for a future match against the same player. Tell your students to keep the comments brief. For example, in the space next to "Forehand," a player might write, "uses topspin on most shots; usually hits crosscourt." A "Style of Play" comment could be, "gets everything back; not a hard hitter."

The *Error Chart* is meant to record how points are lost. When patterns of errors show up on the chart, weaknesses are indicated and may be corrected. For example, if the chart shows that a player is consistently making errors on the first serve, you can suggest less power and better placement. If more than 60% of all errors are made on backhand groundstrokes, you will have a very easy time convincing the player to spend more time working on that weakness.

The *Winning Shot Chart* points out strengths in a player's game and may even give that player confidence to play better. Sometimes players think they can consistently win points on certain shots because those shots are difficult or spectacular. The Winning Shot Chart may, in fact, prove to them that other, less spectacular shots are the ones responsible for winning games and sets.

Whatever the results of charting matches are, writing those results down gives you another tool to help teach and coach players.

Postmatch Scouting Form

Directions: Play a set or a match, then complete this form.

Name of opponent _____ Date of match _____

Results of match: _____ Won, _____ Lost; Score _____

Type of court _____ Weather _____

WRITE ONE OBSERVATION IN EACH CATEGORY ABOUT YOUR OPPONENT

Forehand _____

Backhand _____

First serve _____

Second serve _____

Forehand volley _____

Backhand volley _____

Smash _____

Best shot _____

Weakest shot _____

Speed _____

Strength _____

Quickness _____

Endurance _____

Style of play _____

Right-handed/left-handed _____

Honesty on calls _____

Comments _____

Error Chart

Directions: Tally errors made in each game according to the strokes listed in the left column. For example, if the first serve fails to go into the proper court three times in the first game, mark "III" in the appropriate space.

Game

Stroke	1	2	3	4	5	6	7	8	9
1st serve									
2nd serve									
FH serve return									
BH serve return									
FH groundstroke									
BH groundstroke									
FH volley									
BH volley									
Lob									
Smash									
Drop shot									

Winning Shot Chart

Directions: Tally winning shots during each game according to the strokes listed in the left column.

Game

Stroke	1	2	3	4	5	6	7	8	9
1st serve									
2nd serve									
FH serve return									
BH serve return									
FH groundstroke									
BH groundstroke									
FH volley									
BH volley									
Lob									
Smash									
Drop shot									

Gymnasium and Classroom Activities

You should develop some classroom or gymnasium activities for bad-weather days and to supplement regular outdoor class routines. Save these lessons for inclement weather rather than use them up when the weather is good.

GYMNASIUM ACTIVITIES

1. Ups and Downs *(2 to 40 beginners):* Spread students throughout the gym. Have them practice bouncing the ball up and down using the forehand grip.

2. Dribble Relay *(6 to 40 beginners):* Divide the class into teams. Run relay races using "ups" and "downs," that is, sustained bouncing into the air and off the floor, respectively.

3. Bump Tennis *(2 to 40 beginning or intermediate players):* Pairs of partners face each other across a line on the basketball court at a distance of 15 feet. They keep the ball in play by bumping the ball softly so that it bounces beyond the line separating them.

4. Drop and Hit *(2 to 40 beginners):* Position students around the gym at a distance of 20 feet from the wall. Have them practice dropping the ball and putting it into play against the wall.

5. Wall Groundstrokes *(2 to 40 beginning, intermediate, or advanced players):* Position students around the gym at a distance of 20 feet from the wall. Have them practice forehands and backhands against the wall.

6. Toss to Groundstrokes *(2 to 40 beginners or intermediates):* Have pairs of students stand approximately 20 feet apart. One tosses to the forehand or backhand of the other, who hits controlled groundstrokes back to the tosser. Position tossers with their backs to the wall to stop off-target shots.

7. Alternating Wall Groundstrokes *(2 to 40 beginning, intermediate, or advanced players):* Players in groups of two or three keep the ball in play against the wall from a distance of approximately 20 feet.

8. Team Wall Groundstrokes *(3 to 12 beginning, intermediate, or advanced players per team):* Three or more players stand single file 20 feet or more from a wall. They take turns hitting and keeping the ball in play against the wall.

9. Wall Volleys *(2 to 40 intermediate or advanced players):* Position students around the gym at a distance of 10 to 15 feet from the wall. Have them keep the ball in play by hitting controlled volleys against the wall.

10. Partner Wall Volleys *(2 to 40 intermediate or advanced players):* A pair of players stands 10 to 15 feet from the wall. They alternate hitting volleys off the wall, keeping the ball going.

11. Team Wall Volleys *(3 to 12 intermediate or advanced players per team):* Three or more players in line take turns hitting volleys off the wall, keeping the ball going.

12. Team Volleys *(6 to 12 intermediate or advanced players per team):* Players on two teams stand in lines facing each other at a distance of 15 to 20 feet. They keep the ball in play by hitting volleys to each other.

13. 2-Minute Lobs *(2 to 20 intermediate or advanced players):* Place students around the gym at a distance of at least 30 feet from the wall. Have them practice hitting lobs to a target area on the wall.

14. 2-Minute Overhead Smashes *(2 to 20 intermediate or advanced players):* Place students around the gym at a distance of at least 30 feet from the wall. Have them practice hitting smashes that first hit the floor, then bounce into the wall and up for the next smash.

15. Backboard Drill *(2 to 40 beginning, intermediate, or advanced players):* Position players behind a restraining line. They put the ball in play above a target line on the wall and return as many shots off the wall as possible for 30 seconds. Players may not cross the line to hit the ball, but may to retrieve it.

16. Grounders *(2 to 40 beginning, intermediate, or advanced players):* Partners take turns fielding grounders tossed alternately to the right and the left sides. One player tosses balls while the other fields and rolls them back for a 30-second period.

17. Wave Drill *(2 to 40 beginning, intermediate, or advanced players):* Players spread out facing you. For 30-second periods, you signal them to move forward, backward, left, and right.

18. Run the Lines *(2 to 40 beginning, intermediate, or advanced players):* Players start at the line under and parallel to the basketball backboard. On your ''go'' command, they run forward to the free throw line, backward to the end line, forward to the halfcourt line, backward to the end line, forward to the opposite end free throw line, backward to the end line, and forward all the way to the opposite end line.

19. Shadow Drill *(2 to 40 beginning, intermediate, or advanced players):* Pairs of players face each other at a distance of 15 feet across free throw lines, end lines, sidelines, or halfcourt lines. Designated players move forward, backward, left, or right, while their partners mirror their movements. Change designated players every 30 seconds.

20. Simulated Footwork *(2 intermediate or advanced players at a time):* Two players head up lines of students at the basketball end line. The two simulate service, approach, forehand volley, backhand volley, and smash, then move out of the way for the next players.

CLASSROOM ACTIVITIES

If there is not a gymnasium or fieldhouse facility available for tennis activity classes, reserve a classroom for days when the weather is bad.

Class periods can be designed around the following formats:

Lecture and Discussion

- Rules (singles, doubles)
- Scoring (points, games, sets, matches, no-ad, tiebreakers) [see scoring quiz in Step 7, this book]
- Nutrition (general nutrition, pregame nutrition, weight management)
- Equipment (rackets, strings, balls, shoes, clothes, accessories)
- Fitness (components, benefits, types of exercises, risks)
- Injuries (blisters, sprains, strains, shin splints, tennis elbow)
- Terms (see Glossary in participant's book)
- Strategy (see Steps 15, 16, and 17 in this book)
- Formats for competition (tournaments, individual and team matches, ladders, leagues)
- United States Tennis Association (functions, organization, instructional programs, player development, publications)
- Answers to questions on ''Adjusting to Opponents and Conditions'' (see Step 17, this book)
- Concentration (see Step 18, this book)
- Results of concentration activities in Step 18, participant's book
- Results of Postmatch Scouting Form, Error Chart, and Winning Shot Chart in Step 19, both this book and participant's book

Question-and-Answer Contests

- Refer to the test bank in this book.
- Distribute tennis magazines and develop questions from those publications.

Reading Assignments

- Have students report on the following subjects from magazine articles

    Strokes
    Strategy
    Rules
    Competition
    Tennis personalities
    Facilities
    Issues

Equipment
Instruction programs
Tennis camps, schools, resorts
Prevention and treatment of injuries

• Make reading assignments from these publications

World Tennis
Tennis
Tennis USA
Scholastic Coach
Journal of Physical Education and Recreation

Tennis Films and Videotapes

• USTA Center for Education
  and Recreational Tennis
Publications Department
707 Alexander Road
Princeton, NJ 08540

• American Alliance for Health, Physical
  Education, Recreation, and Dance
Publications Department
1900 Association Drive
Reston, VA 22091

Guest Speakers

• High school coaches
• College coaches
• City program directors
• Tournament directors
• Physical education teachers
• Racket stringers
• Teaching professionals
• USTA volunteers and officers
• Local tournament-level players

The special features in the participant's book, *Tennis: Steps to Success*, provide an ongoing evaluation system. The Keys to Success list aspects of technique that can be subjectively evaluated by a peer, a teacher, or a coach. The points within keys include style of play, fundamentals, movement, and coordination. The Keys to Success presented only in this instructor's book may differ slightly from those in the participant's book; they focus on the whole, fluid combination of movements and body positions involved in playing tennis. "Success Goals" in both books are evaluations of performance that can be measured objectively.

COMBINING QUALITATIVE AND QUANTITATIVE EVALUATION

It is important to combine qualitative and quantitative evaluations in order to cover the various needs and abilities of typical beginning students. By your combining subjective and objective evaluations, students who are inexperienced, overweight, less skilled, or weak will learn that they can improve their grades by using good technique. This should motivate them to practice and improve their performance. Using only quantitative evaluations would reward only the highly skilled, highly conditioned, and experienced students who happen to be taking a beginning course.

AN INDIVIDUAL PROGRAM

See the Sample Individual Program (Appendix C.1) for an example of an individual evaluation system that uses both technique and performance objectives. The list is comprehensive, so few instructors would have the time to test their students on all of the criteria. A blank program sheet (Appendix C.2) is available for you to fill in your own system of grading. To create an individual program, decide on these four things: (a) the total number of skills and concepts to be measured; (b) the specific subjective criteria to be observed; (c) the weight to be placed on any skill or concept (based on available practice time and degree of difficulty); and (d) the type of grading system you prefer (letters, numbers, percentages, etc.)

In tennis, it is possible and desirable to determine a grade for technique as well as accuracy. For example, a student may demonstrate the correct technique (form) for hitting a full-swing serve, but in a skill test for the serve, that student may do very poorly. Another student may violate every rule of good technique in serving, but hit 10 serves out of 10 attempts into the proper court. By weighing and evaluating both variables—technique and accuracy—the student is given a fair chance to demonstrate his or her ability. Technique objectives for the full-swing serve include (a) Continental grip, (b) rhythmic swing, (c) extended arm and body at contact, and (d) complete follow-through. A performance objective asks the student to place 1–5 full-swing serves into the proper court.

ADAPTING INDIVIDUAL PROGRAMS

If you are working with very large classes of students in three or more grade levels, select only four to six major objectives. There will not be enough time or space for comprehensive mastery or testing to see whether objectives have been reached. Include some opportunities for self-testing, but structure the remaining tests so that the skills to be measured are based on the self-test skills. This will provide a check-and-balance system of evaluating a few important skills. The Sample Group Program (Appendix C.3) gives examples of the most important and easiest skills to measure in a group setting.

A second Skill Test Form is shown in Figure E.1. The students are tested on eight skills, valued from 1 to 10 points, and on general hitting ability, valued from 1 to 20 points. The first eight skills are measured by having the student accurately hit into target areas, but you may add or subtract points, depending on the technique used in executing the strokes. The general hitting measures give the student a chance to earn points by keeping the ball in play, hitting and moving, and using correct technique. All points are earned during skill tests at the end of the semester or series of classes.

The final skill grade may be decided by a predetermined grading scale or the scores may be curved for the group's skill level. The advantage of grading by a predetermined scale is that the students know exactly what is expected of them when the course begins. The disadvantage of this system is that it is possible for an entire group of students to be above or below average in their skills. The final distribution of grades could be very high or very low. The advantages of curving grades are that students have a better sense of comparing their skills to others in the class, and the instructor can make adjustments in the curve based on the collective ability of the students in each class.

In both systems, each student can earn a maximum of 100 points ($8 \times 10 + 20$), making the grading scale consistent with other disciplines and familiar to the student. In larger classes, save time by using 5 trials instead of 10. Also, consider using only the first skills plus the general hitting score to determine grades; in beginning classes the smash, the lob, and the drop shot may require more time to develop than is available and may have to be omitted.

Whichever evaluation system you select, it is helpful to distribute your evaluation program sheets at the beginning of your course. Then your students will know exactly what is expected of them. They can practice grading each other, and they can become accustomed to performing under pressure.

Figure E.1 Skill Test Form

Name	Forehand	Backhand	Punch serve	Full serve	Volley	Smash	Lob	Drop	General	Total	Grade
Example	10	7	9	7	8	7	7	5	20	80	B

Test Bank

The following questions cover a range of tennis information on rules, strokes, and strategy. Select questions appropriate for the level being taught and reflecting content that has been covered.

RULES

Directions: Write the letter corresponding to the correct answer for each question in the blank provided.

_____ 1. The height of the net at the center is
   a. 1-1/2 racket lengths.
   b. 3 feet.
   c. 3-1/2 feet.
   d. 4 feet.

_____ 2. The warm-up period before a match should not last more than
   a. 5 minutes.
   b. 10 minutes.
   c. 2 minutes.
   d. no limit.

_____ 3. At the beginning of a match, the winner of the racket spin may
   a. choose only to serve or receive.
   b. choose only to serve, receive, or begin play on a particular side.
   c. choose to serve, receive, or begin on a particular side, or ask the opponent to choose.
   d. choose both the side on which to begin play and the order of serving.

_____ 4. Practice serves can be taken
   a. before each player serves the first time.
   b. during the warm-up before the first point of the match.
   c. at the beginning of each set.
   d. any time during the match, as long as the opponent is notified.

_____ 5. In no-ad scoring, from which side does the server serve the seventh point?
   a. the server decides
   b. the right side
   c. the left side
   d. the receiver decides

_____ 6. In regular scoring, 30–40 means
   a. the server is winning.
   b. the receiver is winning.
   c. either player could be winning.
   d. the winner of the next point wins the game.

_____ 7. What is the score when the server loses the point after deuce?
   a. ad out
   b. ad in
   c. game to the receiver
   d. game to the server

_____ 8. What determines whether the receiver is ready to return a serve?
   a. The receiver makes eye contact with the server.
   b. The server serves, the receiver has to be ready.
   c. The server asks the receiver whether he or she is ready.
   d. The receiver attempts to return the serve.

_____ 9. Which statement is true?
   a. An underhand service motion is a fault.
   b. It is a fault if a server swings and misses a toss.
   c. It is a fault if a server tosses the ball, then catches it.
   d. It is legal to drop the ball, then serve it off the bounce.

_____ 10. When a team is receiving a first serve, who may call the serve out?
   a. only the receiver
   b. only the receiver's partner
   c. either the receiver or the receiver's partner
   d. the server or the server's partner

_____ 11. What happens if a ball rolls onto the court between the first and second serves?
   a. A let should be called if there is an unusual delay.
   b. A let should be called if the server asks for it.
   c. The server serves the second ball.
   d. A let should be called automatically.

_____ 12. Which statement is true?
   a. A player may reach over the net to hit a ball after it has bounced on his or her side of the court.
   b. A player may not reach over the net to hit a ball.
   c. A player may touch the net with his racket after hitting the ball.
   d. A player may reach over the net to hit a ball if the wind slows the ball down.

_____ 13. What happens if a player returns a ball that passes outside the net post below the level of the top of the net and into the opponent's court?
   a. A let is played.
   b. The player who hits the shot loses the point.
   c. The ball is in play.
   d. The player who hits the shot wins the point.

_____ 14. What happens when a shot obviously going out is caught by a player standing behind the baseline?
   a. The point is replayed.
   b. The player who hits the ball loses the point.
   c. The player who catches the ball wins the point.
   d. The player who catches the ball loses the point.

_____ 15. On a shot that hits the line, the person on whose side the ball bounces should
   a. call the shot "good" and continue playing.
   b. call a let.
   c. call the ball out.
   d. say nothing and continue playing.

_____ 16. What happens if a player serves from the wrong side in singles?
   a. The point counts and the next point is played from the proper court.
   b. The point is replayed.
   c. The point counts, and the server continues serving from the wrong court until the game is over.
   d. The server forfeits that game.

_____ 17. What happens when doubles partners play a point after having lined up on the wrong sides?
    a. If the receiving team makes the error, the point stands, and the correction is made at the end of the game.
    b. The point is replayed.
    c. The team that makes the error loses the point.
    d. If the receiving team makes the error, the point stands, and the correction is made immediately.

_____ 18. What happens if a ball rolls onto the court while a point is in progress?
    a. The point automatically stops.
    b. Only the player on whose side the ball has rolled may call a let.
    c. The point continues.
    d. Either player may call a let if the call is made immediately.

_____ 19. On a disputed call, who has the final word?
    a. the coach
    b. the players involved
    c. anyone who has a good view of the shot in question
    d. the point is automatically replayed

_____ 20. When should players change ends of the court?
    a. after every game
    b. after every set
    c. when the total number of games played is an even number
    d. when the total number of games played is an odd number

_____ 21. How much time do you have to rest when changing ends of the court?
    a. 1-1/2 minutes
    b. 1 minute
    c. 2 minutes
    d. 5 minutes

_____ 22. What is the minimum amount of time you have to rest between matches?
    a. 15 minutes
    b. 30 minutes
    c. 1 hour
    d. 1-1/2 hours

_____ 23. When in doubt about whether a shot is good or out
    a. play the shot as if it were good.
    b. call a let.
    c. call it out.
    d. ask a spectator to call the shot.

_____ 24. If a player becomes ill during a match, how much time is allowed for recovery?
    a. 2 minutes
    b. 5 minutes
    c. no time is allowed
    d. as much time as the player needs

_____ 25. When can doubles partners change the order of receiving serve?
    a. at the end of any game
    b. at the end of any set
    c. no change allowed
    d. at any time, as long as the opponents are notified

_____ 26. When can doubles partners change the order of serving?
   a. at the end of any set
   b. at any time, as long as the opponents are notified
   c. no change allowed
   d. at the end of any game

_____ 27. What is the USTA rule on coaching during team matches?
   a. No coaching is allowed.
   b. Coaches can talk to players at any time.
   c. Coaching is allowed when play will not be interrupted.
   d. Coaching is allowed if the player initiates the contact.

_____ 28. In a 12-point tiebreaker, a player must
   a. win 12 points.
   b. win 7 points.
   c. win 6 points.
   d. win 7 points and be ahead by at least 2 points.

_____ 29. Who begins serving a 12-point tiebreaker?
   a. the player who would have served the next game
   b. the players who won a new spin for serve
   c. the player who served the last game before the tiebreaker
   d. the player who lost the racket spin at the beginning of the match

_____ 30. When do players change ends of the court during a tiebreaker?
   a. after the total number of points played is an odd number
   b. after every 6 points
   c. before the next set begins
   d. after every 6 points and before the next set begins

STROKES

Directions: Write the letter corresponding to the correct answer for each question in the blank provided.

_____ 1. What is the position of the wrist in an Eastern forehand grip?
   a. slightly to the right of the top bevel of the grip (right-handed player)
   b. slightly to the left of the top bevel of the grip (right-handed player)
   c. directly on top of the top bevel of the grip
   d. changes with the position of the ball

_____ 2. The Continental grip is recommended for the
   a. forehand groundstroke.
   b. backhand groundstroke.
   c. beginner's serve.
   d. advanced volley.

_____ 3. On which of the following shots should the racket be held tighter?
   a. volleys
   b. drop shots
   c. groundstrokes
   d. lobs

_____ 4. How far back should the racket be brought in preparation for a groundstroke?
   a. as far as is comfortable
   b. no more than 2 feet behind the body
   c. there is no guideline for a backswing
   d. until pointing to the fence or wall behind you

_____ 5. How far back should the racket be brought in preparation for a volley?
   a. as far as in comfortable
   b. no more than 2 feet behind your body
   c. there is no guideline for a backswing
   d. until pointing to the fence or wall behind you

_____ 6. For which kind of shot should a crossover step be used?
   a. a groundstroke for which you to have to run several steps
   b. a groundstroke that comes directly at your body
   c. a groundstroke that comes slightly to your right or left
   d. an overhead smash

_____ 7. Which is the proper grip for a beginner's serve?
   a. Eastern forehand
   b. Eastern backhand
   c. Continental
   d. Western forehand

_____ 8. What is the advantage of a Continental grip on volleys?
   a. It is more comfortable.
   b. It gives you more power.
   c. It is the natural way to hold the racket.
   d. You save time by not having to change grips.

_____ 9. How high should a toss be made for a serve?
   a. about 18 inches
   b. slightly higher than you can reach with your racket
   c. as high as is comfortable for you
   d. just high enough to reach the middle of your racket strings when your arm is extended

_____ 10. In a forehand or backhand groundstroke, where should the racket's follow-through be completed?
   a. pointing in the direction of the shot
   b. stopping at the point of contact
   c. wrapping around the front of your body
   d. pointing down at the court

_____ 11. What is a half-volley?
   a. a volley hit with a half-swinging motion
   b. a groundstroke hit in the middle of the court
   c. a ball hit immediately after it bounces on the court
   d. a weakly hit volley

_____ 12. Which statement about the drop shot is correct?
   a. Swing from low to high.
   b. Hit it with topspin.
   c. Hold the racket tighter than usual.
   d. Swing from high to low.

_____ 13. Not following through on a groundstroke might cause
   a. the ball to sail out.
   b. a lack of power.
   c. tennis elbow.
   d. too much spin on the ball.

_____ 14. On which shot should the racket face be open slightly to the sky?
   a. serve
   b. forehand groundstroke
   c. smash
   d. lob

_____ 15. The position of the racket to begin a punch serve is
   a. in front of your body.
   b. out to the side of your body.
   c. in front of your face.
   d. behind your head.

_____ 16. The point of contact on an overhead smash is
   a. high and in front of your body.
   b. directly over your head.
   c. slightly behind your head.
   d. in front of your face.

_____ 17. Letting the ball drop too low on serves and smashes will probably cause
   a. the ball to sail deep.
   b. the ball to go to the right or left.
   c. the ball to go into the net.
   d. you to take your eyes off the ball.

_____ 18. When a right-hander keeps hitting the ball to the right of the opponent's court, the problem is probably
   a. a backswing that is too short.
   b. holding the racket with the wrong grip.
   c. turning the side to the net.
   d. preparing for the shot too late.

_____ 19. Stepping forward on volleys provides
   a. power.
   b. control.
   c. spin on the ball.
   d. more time to react.

_____ 20. Having the body's weight on the back foot can cause
   a. inconsistency.
   b. more power.
   c. a lack of power.
   d. foot injuries.

_____ 21. The follow-through on serves should be
   a. down, out, and across.
   b. out, across, and down.
   c. across and down.
   d. up and out toward the net.

_____ 22. The two-handed backhand is
     a. for children and beginners.
     b. used by players at all levels.
     c. one that has no disadvantages.
     d. better than a one-handed backhand.

_____ 23. The position of the body to begin the serving motion is
     a. facing the net.
     b. standing at a right angle to the baseline.
     c. standing at a 45-degree angle to the baseline.
     d. standing in the position that feels the most comfortable.

_____ 24. On which shots does the elbow bend the most during the swing?
     a. forehand volleys
     b. backhand groundstrokes
     c. half-volleys
     d. full-swing serve

_____ 25. On which shots should the wrist remain in a fixed position?
     a. groundstrokes
     b. serves
     c. smashes
     d. all strokes

_____ 26. What is the position of the tossing arm before a full-swing serve?
     a. to the side of the body
     b. pointing in the direction you want to serve
     c. pointing slightly to the left of where you want to serve
     d. at your side

_____ 27. On groundstrokes and volleys, in which direction should you step with the foot opposite your racket arm?
     a. across, in the direction the ball is coming
     b. in the direction you want to hit
     c. away from the ball, in order to set up
     d. toward the net post

_____ 28. A short backswing on any line stroke
     a. is desirable.
     b. can give control but can cause a lack of power.
     c. can give power but can cause a lack of control.
     d. is a mistake.

_____ 29. Contact with the ball on volleys should be made
     a. while the ball is still rising.
     b. as the ball descends.
     c. as the ball gets even with the side of your body.
     d. with a loose grip.

_____ 30. When you have less time than normal to prepare for any shot
     a. lengthen your backswing.
     b. swing harder.
     c. lob.
     d. shorten your backswing.

STRATEGY

Directions. Write the letter corresponding to the correct answer for each question in the blank provided.

_____   1. Following most shots,
     a. return to the middle of the court.
     b. return to the middle of the baseline.
     c. wait to see where your opponent's next shot will go.
     d. go to the net.

_____   2. Direct most serves
     a. to the forehand.
     b. to the backhand.
     c. directly at the receiver.
     d. to a weakness or an open area.

_____   3. The most effective serves
     a. are the hardest hit ones.
     b. are ones hit with medium pace to a specific target area.
     c. have spin on the ball.
     d. are hit into the forehand court.

_____   4. When returning the serve, stand
     a. near the baseline, near the singles sideline.
     b. just behind the service line.
     c. at the center mark on the baseline.
     d. in a position that protects your backhand.

_____   5. Most groundstrokes should be hit
     a. crosscourt and deep.
     b. down the line.
     c. down the middle of the court.
     d. to your opponent's backhand.

_____   6. Volleys used to return shots hit down the line should be hit
     a. down the line.
     b. down the middle.
     c. crosscourt.
     d. so that they drop in front of your opponent.

_____   7. Volleys used to return shots hit crosscourt should be hit
     a. down the line.
     b. down the middle.
     c. crosscourt.
     d. deep and back to your opponent.

_____   8. During a baseline rally,
     a. develop a pattern and stay with it.
     b. develop a pattern and break it.
     c. hit only to the opponent's backhand.
     d. hit only crosscourt shots.

_____   9. Try to put away shots with an overhead smash
     a. from the backcourt.
     b. from the area behind your baseline.
     c. from the forecourt.
     d. at every opportunity.

_____ 10. Drop shots
   a. should not be tried from the baseline.
   b. are effective against players who can cover the court well.
   c. are effective with the wind at your back.
   d. should not be used by recreational players.

_____ 11. Lobs
   a. are not effective in singles.
   b. can be used offensively and defensively.
   c. should be used as a last-resort shot.
   d. are effective when you are in a forecourt position.

_____ 12. When you are serving in doubles, stand
   a. near the center mark
   b. behind the doubles alley.
   c. approximately halfway between the center mark and the doubles sideline.
   d. in a position to protect your backhand.

_____ 13. When a shot goes between you and your partner
   a. the player with the strongest backhand should take the shot.
   b. the player with the forehand should take the shot.
   c. call for the shot first, then hit it.
   d. use a lob to return the shot.

_____ 14. When both opponents are at the net and you are on the baseline
   a. lob to the right side.
   b. consider the drop shot.
   c. hit low and down the middle.
   d. go to the net.

_____ 15. In doubles, when your opponent serves and stays back
   a. hit crosscourt and short.
   b. hit at the net player.
   c. return the ball and hold your position.
   d. return crosscourt and deep.

_____ 16. When your partner moves off the court to retrieve a shot,
   a. shift slightly in that direction.
   b. drop straight back to the baseline.
   c. hold your position.
   d. protect your alley.

_____ 17. When you poach
   a. concentrate on keeping the ball in play.
   b. go for a winner.
   c. hit back to the receiver.
   d. hit a drop shot.

_____ 18. When playing on slow courts,
   a. go for winners more often.
   b. plan on short points and sets.
   c. be patient.
   d. go to the net more often.

_____ 19. When playing against hard hitters,
    a. play a step deeper on service returns.
    b. remember to fight power with power.
    c. pick up the pace of the match.
    d. go to the net at every opportunity.

_____ 20. If you are losing,
    a. think about the next match.
    b. change strategy.
    c. pick up the pace of the match.
    d. talk to yourself between points.

_____ 21. Take chances when
    a. you can afford to lose points.
    b. the score is close.
    c. you are tired.
    d. you are playing a left-hander.

TEST BANK ANSWERS

Rules	Strokes	Strategy
1. b	1. a	1. b
2. a	2. d	2. d
3. c	3. a	3. b
4. b	4. d	4. a
5. d	5. b	5. a
6. b	6. a	6. c
7. a	7. a	7. a
8. d	8. d	8. b
9. b	9. b	9. c
10. c	10. a	10. a
11. a	11. c	11. b
12. a	12. d	12. c
13. c	13. b	13. b
14. d	14. d	14. c
15. d	15. d	15. d
16. a	16. a	16. a
17. a	17. c	17. b
18. d	18. d	18. c
19. b	19. a	19. a
20. d	20. c	20. b
21. a	21. b	21. a
22. a	22. b	
23. a	23. c	
24. c	24. d	
25. b	25. a	
26. a	26. b	
27. a	27. b	
28. d	28. b	
29. a	29. a	
30. b	30. d	

Appendices

A   Knowledge Structure of Tennis (Overview)
B.1 Sample Scope and Teaching Sequence
B.2 Scope and Teaching Sequence (Blank)
C.1 Sample Individual Program
C.2 Individual Program (Blank)
C.3 Sample Group Program
D.1 Sample Lesson Plan
D.2 Lesson Plan (Blank)

Appendix A
How to Use the Knowledge Structure (Overview)

A knowledge structure is an instructional tool—by completing one you make a very personal statement about what you know about a subject and how that knowledge guides your decisions in teaching and coaching. The Knowledge Structure of Tennis outlined here has been designed for a teaching environment, with teaching progressions that emphasize technique and performance objectives in realistic settings. In a coaching environment, you would need to emphasize more physiological and conditioning factors with training progressions that prepare athletes for competition.

The Knowledge Structure of Tennis shows the first page or an *overview* of a completed knowledge structure. The knowledge structure is divided into broad categories of information that are used for all of the participant and instructor guides in the Steps to Success Activity Series. Those categories are

- physiological training and conditioning,
- background knowledge,
- psychomotor skills and tactics, and
- psycho-social concepts.

Physiological training and conditioning has several subcategories, including warm-up and cool-down. Research in exercise physiology and the medical sciences has demonstrated the importance of warming up and cooling down after physical activity. The participant and instructor guides present principles and exercises for effective warm-up and cool-down, which, because of time restrictions, are usually the only training activities done in the teaching environment. In a more intense coaching environment, additional categories should be added—training principles, injury prevention, training progressions, and nutrition principles.

The background-knowledge category presents sub-categories of information that represent essential background knowledges that all instructors should command when meeting their classes. For tennis, background knowledge includes playing the game, basic rules/safety, equipment, tennis today, and tennis injuries.

Under psychomotor skills and tactics, all the individual skills in an activity are named. For tennis, these are shown as racket handling, preparing to hit, groundstrokes, serve, beginner's volley, lob, smash, advanced volley, half-volley, and drop shot. These skills are also presented in a recommended order of presentation. In a completed knowledge structure, each skill is broken down into subskills, delineating selected technical, biomechanical, motor learning, and other teaching and coaching points that describe mature performance. These points can be found in the Student Keys to Success or in the Keys to Success Checklists within the participant book.

Once individual skills are identified and analyzed, then selected basic tactics of the activity are also identified and analyzed. For tennis, both offensive and defensive tactics include singles, doubles, mixed doubles, playing conditions, and concentration. Notice that they are arranged to reflect the decision making strategies and capabilities of learners as they become more proficient.

The psycho-social category identifies selected concepts from the sports psychology and sociology literature that have been shown to contribute to the learners' understanding of and success in the activity. These concepts are built into the key concepts and activities for teaching. For tennis, the concept identified is concentration.

To be a successful teacher or coach, you must convert what you have learned as a student or done as a player or performer to knowledge that is conscious and appropriate for presentation to others. A knowledge structure is a tool designed to help you with this transition and to speed your *steps to success*. You should view a knowledge structure as the most basic level of teaching knowledge you possess for a sport or activity. For more information on how to develop your own knowledge structure, see the textbook that accompanies this series, *Instructional Design for Teaching Physical Activities*.

Knowledge Structure of Tennis (Overview)

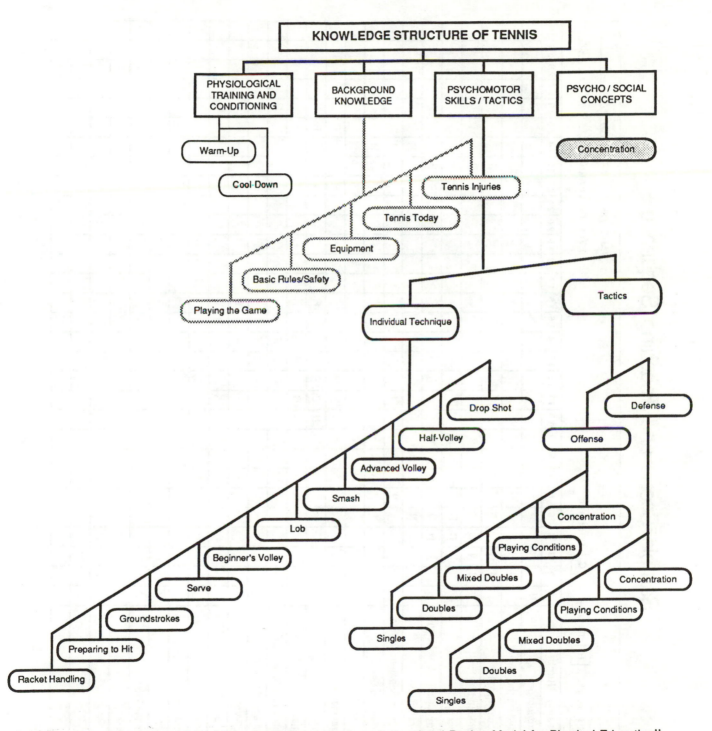

Note. From "The Role of Expert Knowledge Structures in an Instructional Design Model for Physical Education" by J.N. Vickers, 1983, *Journal of Teaching in Physical Education*, 2(3), pp. 25, 27. Copyright 1983 by Joan N. Vickers. Adapted by permission. This Knowledge Structure of Tennis was designed specifically for the Steps to Success Activity Series by Joan N. Vickers, Judy P. Wright, and Jim Brown.

Appendix B.1

Sample Scope and Teaching Sequence

NAME OF ACTIVITY: *Tennis*
LEVEL OF LEARNER: *Beginning – Int.*

Legend: **N** = New **R** = Review **C** = Continue

Steps	Session Number	1	2	3	4	5	6	7	8	9	10	11	12	13	14	15	16	17	18	19	20	21	22	23	24	25	26	27	28	29	30
	Introduction	N																													
1	Handling the Racket		N	R																											
2	Preparing to Hit		N	C																			R								
3	Forehand		N	N	C	R																		R							
3	Backhand			N	C	R																		R							
4	Groundstroke Combinations				N	C																		R							
5	Punch Serve					N	C	R																	R						
—	Rules, Equipment, Terms						N																		R						
6	Full-Swing Serve							N	C	R															R						
7	3 Shot Singles							N	C	C																					
8	Beginner's Volley								N	C	R						R									R					
9	Lob									N	C	R					R									R					
10	Smash									N	C	R					R									R					
11	Volley-Lob-Smash Comb.											N	C	R													R				
12	Advanced Volley												N	C	R												R				
13	Half-Volley													N	C	R	R										R				
14	Drop Shot														N	C	C										R				
15	Singles																	N	C	C											
16	Doubles																				N	C	C								
	Skills Tests																											N	N	N	
	Written Test																														N

Notes:

Appendix B.2
How to Use the Scope and Teaching Sequence Form

A completed Scope and Teaching Sequence is, in effect, a master lesson plan. It lists all the individual skills to be included in your course, recorded (vertically) in the progressive sequence in which you have decided to present them and showing (horizontally) the manner and the sessions in which you teach them.

The Sample Scope and Teaching Sequence illustrates how the chart is to be used. This chart indicates that in session 9, the class will review the Full-Swing Serve (Step 6), continue playing Three-Shot Singles (Step 7), and be introduced to the Beginner's Volley (Step 8). It also indicates that the skills in Step 7 (Three-Shot Singles), for example, are worked on for three sessions—one introduction and two continuations.

A course Scope and Teaching Sequence chart (use the blank form in Appendix B.2) will help you to better plan your daily teaching strategies (see Appendix D.1). It will take some experience to predict accurately how much material you can cover in each session, but by completing a plan like this, you can compare your progress to your plan and revise the plan to better fit the next class.

The chart will also help you tailor the amount of material to the length of time you have to teach it. Be sure that your course's Scope and Teaching Sequence allots ample time for review and practice of each area.

Remember that the Scope and Teaching Sequence can be affected by the number of students in a class, the collective abilities of your students, the number of courts and tennis balls available, and the weather. While the one presented here or the one you complete for yourself can serve as guides, it is very difficult to follow either of them exactly. Be ready to make adjustments according to the variables mentioned.

Appendix B.2

Scope and Teaching Sequence

| N | New | | R | Review | | C | Continue |

NAME OF ACTIVITY _____

LEVEL OF LEARNER _____

Steps	Session Number	1	2	3	4	5	6	7	8	9	10	11	12	13	14	15	16	17	18	19	20	21	22	23	24	25	26	27	28	29	30
1																																
2																																
3																																
4																																
5																																
6																																
7																																
8																																
9																																
10																																
11																																
12																																
13																																
14																																
15																																
16																																
17																																
18																																
19																																
20																																
21																																
22																																
23																																
24																																
25																																

Note. From *Badminton: A Structures of Knowledge Approach* (pp. 60-61) by J.N. Vickers and D. Brecht, 1987, Calgary, AB: University Printing Services. Copyright 1987 by Joan N. Vickers. Adapted by permission.

Appendix C.1
How to Use the Individual Program Form

To complete an individual program for each student, you must first make five decisions about evaluation:

1. How many skills or concepts can you or should you evaluate, considering the number of students and the time available? The larger your classes and the shorter your class length, the fewer objectives you will be able to use.

2. What specific quantitative or qualitative criteria will you use to evaluate specific skills? See the Sample Individual Program (Appendix C.1) for ideas.

3. What relative weight is to be assigned to each specific skill, considering its importance in the course and the amount of practice time available?

4. What type of grading system do you wish to use? Will you use letters (A, B, C, D), satisfactory/unsatisfactory, a number or point system (1, 2, 3, etc.), or percentages (10%, 20%, 30%, etc.)? Or you may prefer a system of achievement levels, such as colors (red, white, blue), creatures (panthers, lions, tigers), or medallions (gold, silver, bronze).

5. Who will do the evaluating? You may want to delegate certain quantitative evaluations to be made by the students' peers up to a predetermined skill level (e.g., a ''B'' grade), with all qualitative evaluations and all top-grade determinations being made by you.

Once you have made these decisions, draw up an evaluation sheet (using Appendix C.2) that will fit the majority of your class members. Then decide whether you will establish a minimum level as a passing/failing point. Calculate the minimum passing score and the maximum attainable score, and divide the difference into as many grade categories as you wish. If you use an achievement-level system, assign a numerical value to each level for your calculations.

The blank Individual Program form, as shown in Appendix C.2, is intended not to be used verbatim (although you may do so if you wish), but rather to suggest ideas that you can use, adapt, and integrate with your own ideas to tailor your program to you and your students. One modification for working with large groups is to reduce the number of technique and performance objectives to be evaluated (see Appendix C.3).

Make copies of your program evaluation system to hand out to each student at your first class meeting, and be prepared to make modifications for those who need special consideration. Such modifications could be changing the weight assigned to particular skills for certain students, or substituting some skills for others, or varying the criteria used for evaluating selected students. Thus, individual differences can be recognized within your class.

You, the instructor, have the freedom to make the decisions about evaluating your students. Be creative. The best teachers always are.

Appendix C.1

Sample Individual Program

INDIVIDUAL COURSE IN ___Tennis___

GRADE/COURSE SECTION _____

STUDENT'S NAME _____

STUDENT ID # _____

SKILLS/CONCEPTS	TECHNIQUE AND PERFORMANCE OBJECTIVES	WT* x	POINT PROGRESS**				= FINAL SCORE***
			1 D	2 C	3 B	4 A	
1 Ready position	*Technique:* Racket and weight forward; opposite hand supporting racket; knees slightly bent.	1					
2 Forehand grip	*Technique:* Wrist slightly to right of top racket handle bevel	1					
3 Forehand	*Technique:* Racket back, pointing to fence; side to net; step forward; parallel swing; steady wrist; early contact; finish pointing to target	1					
	Performance: Of 10 balls tossed or hit to student at baseline, number returned into singles court	1	1-3	4-5	6-7	8-10	
4 Backhand grip	*Technique:* Wrist slightly to left of top racket handle bevel, or two forehand grips with hands touching (for two-handed backhand)	1					
5 Backhand	*Technique:* Racket back, pointing to fence; side to net; step forward; parallel swing; early contact; finish pointing to target	1					
	Performance: Of 10 balls tossed or hit to student at baseline, number returned into singles court	1	1-3	4-5	6-7	8-10	
6 Punch serve	*Technique:* Forehand grip; racket starts behind head; toss up and forward; reach high to hit; follow through out, across, down	1					
	Performance: Of 10 trials, number served into opposite service court	1	1-3	4-5	6-7	8-10	
7 Full-swing serve	*Technique:* Continental grip; rhythmic swing; extend to hit; medium pace on ball; follow through out, across, down	1					
	Performance: Of 5 trials, number served into opposite service court	2	1-2	3	4	5	

SKILLS/CONCEPTS	TECHNIQUE AND PERFORMANCE OBJECTIVES	WT* ×	POINT PROGRESS**				= FINAL SCORE***
			1 D	2 C	3 B	4 A	
8 Beginning volley	*Technique:* Short backswing; forehand or backhand grip (changing); opposite foot forward; contact at side	1					
	Performance: Of 10 balls tossed from service line or hit from baseline, number volleyed into singles court	1	1-3	4-5	6-7	8-10	
9 Advanced volley	*Technique:* Continental grip; short backswing; opposite foot forward; quick recovery	1					
	Performance: Of 5 balls fed from baseline, number volleyed into singles court	2	1-2	3	4	5	
10 Smash	*Technique:* Racket back, early; Continental grip; side to net; extend to hit	1					
	Performance: Of 5 trials, number smashed into singles court	2	1-2	3	4	5	
11 Lob	*Performance:* Of 5 trials, number lobbed into backcourt	2	1-2	3	4	5	
12 Drop shot	*Performance:* Of 5 trials, number dropped into opposite service court (must bounce twice inside service court)	2					
13 General hitting	*Technique:* Early preparation; balance; smooth strokes; ease of movement; anticipation of shots; recovery for next shot	5					

*WT = Weighting of an objective's degree of difficulty

**PROGRESS = Ongoing success, which may be expressed in terms of (a) accumulated points (1, 2, 3, 4); (b) grades (D, C, B, A); (c) symbols (merit, bronze, silver, gold); (d) unsatisfactory/satisfactory; and others as desired.

***FINAL SCORE equals WT times PROGRESS

Appendix C.2

Individual Program

INDIVIDUAL COURSE IN _____

STUDENT'S NAME _____

GRADE/COURSE SECTION _____

STUDENT ID # _____

SKILLS/CONCEPTS	TECHNIQUE AND PERFORMANCE OBJECTIVES	WT* ×	POINT PROGRESS**				=	FINAL SCORE***
			1	2	3	4		

Note. From ''The Role of Expert Knowledge Structures in an Instructional Design Model for Physical Education'' by J.N. Vickers, 1983, *Journal of Teaching in Physical Education, 2*(3), p. 17. Copyright 1983 by Joan N. Vickers. Adapted by permission.

*WT = Weighting of an objective's degree of difficulty.

**PROGRESS = Ongoing success, which may be expressed in terms of (a) accumulated points (1, 2, 3, 4); (b) grades (D, C, B, A); (c) symbols (merit, bronze, silver, gold); (d) unsatisfactory/satisfactory; and others as desired.

***FINAL SCORE equals WT times PROGRESS.

Appendix C.3

Sample Group Program

INDIVIDUAL COURSE IN ___Tennis___

STUDENT'S NAME _____

GRADE/COURSE SECTION _____

STUDENT ID # _____

	SKILLS/CONCEPTS	TECHNIQUE AND PERFORMANCE OBJECTIVES	WT* ×	POINT PROGRESS** =				FINAL SCORE***
				1	2	3	4	
				D	C	B	A	
1	Forehand accuracy	Of 10 trials, number into singles court	1	1-3	4-5	6-7	8-10	
2	Backhand accuracy	Of 10 trials, number into singles court	1	1-3	4-5	6-7	8-10	
3	Punch serve accuracy	Of 10 trials, number into opposite service court	1	1-3	4-5	6-7	8-10	
4	Full serve accuracy	Of 5 trials, number into opposite service court	2	1-2	3	4	5	
5	Beginning volley accuracy	Of 10 trials, number into singles court (mixed FH/BH)	1	1-3	4-5	6-7	8-10	
6	General hitting	Early preparation; balance; smooth strokes; ease of movement; anticipation of shots; recovery for next shot	5					

*WT = Weighting of an objective's degree of difficulty.
**PROGRESS = Ongoing success, which may be expressed in terms of (a) accumulated points (1, 2, 3, 4); (b) grades (D, C, B, A); (c) symbols (merit, bronze, silver, gold); (d) unsatisfactory/satisfactory; and others as desired.
***FINAL SCORE equals WT times PROGRESS.

Appendix D.1
Sample Lesson Plan

Lesson plan _____2_____ of _____30_____ Activity _____Beginning Tennis_____

Class _____10:00–10:50 MWF (30 students)_____

Objectives:

1. Student demonstrates the Eastern forehand grip;
2. Student demonstrates the forehand preparation, swing, and follow-through; and
3. Student drops and hits forehand shots into the opposite court.

Equipment needed:

Tennis rackets and at least three balls per student

Skill or concept	Learning activity	Teaching points	Time (min)
1. Introduce two warm-up activities, and outline objectives of class.	• Court jog (see ''Class Warm-ups'' section, Activity 1) • Side to side (see ''Class Warm-ups'' section, Activity 2)	• Establish the exact time warm-up drills will begin in subsequent classes. • Watch for students who may need special attention in movement drills.	5
2. Demonstrate and check students' Eastern forehand grips.	• Position students apart on the baseline and service lines. Students watch teacher demo and hold rackets with forehand grips.	• Explain the position of the wrist in relation to top of racket handle (slightly to the right for right-handers, to the left for left-handers).	5
3. Lead class in the ''ready, pivot, step, swing'' drill. Face the class while talking and hitting.	• Forehand swings (see Step 3, Drill 1)	• Rackets pointing forward; weight on balls of feet; arms away from body; racket back to fence with forward step; level swing; hold the follow-through.	10
4. Divide class into groups for Drop and Hit Drill.	• Drop and hit (see Step 3, Drill 2)	• Extend the arm to the side to drop the ball; drop it— don't bounce it; shorten backswing, if necessary; move the racket through a ''tunnel'' of air before, during, and after hit.	10
5. Review questions, bridge to next lesson.			

Appendix D.2
How to Use the Lesson Plan Form

All teachers have learned in their training that lesson plans are vital to good teaching. This is a commonly accepted axiom, but there are many variations in the form that lesson plans can take.

An effective lesson plan sets forth the objectives to be attained or attempted during the session. If there is no objective, then there is no reason for teaching, and no basis for judging whether the teaching is effective.

Once you have named your objectives, list specific activities that will lead to attaining each. Every activity must be described in detail—what will take place and in what order, and how the class will be organized for the optimum learning situation. Record key words or phrases as focal points as well as brief reminders of the applicable safety precautions; for example, tell your students to watch for flying tennis balls, rackets being swung, and tennis balls that can be stepped on.

Finally, set a time schedule that allocates a segment of the lesson for each activity to guide you in keeping to your plan. It is wise to also include in your lesson plan a list of all the teaching and safety equipment you will need, as well as a reminder to check for availability and location of the equipment before class.

An organized, professional approach to teaching requires preparing daily lesson plans. Each lesson plan provides you with an effective overview of your intended instruction and a means to evaluate it when class is over. Having lesson plans on file allows someone else to teach in your absence.

You may modify the blank Lesson Plan form shown in Appendix D.2 to fit your own needs, just as I have modified it in the sample to include an equipment list.

Appendix D.2
Lesson Plan

LESSON PLAN _____ OF _____	OBJECTIVES:
ACTIVITY _____	
CLASS _____	

SKILL OR CONCEPT	LEARNING ACTIVITIES	TEACHING POINTS	TIME

Note. From *Badminton: A Structures of Knowledge Approach* (p. 95) by J.N. Vickers and D. Brecht, 1987, Calgary, AB: University Printing Services. Copyright 1987 by Joan N. Vickers. Reprinted by permission.

References

Goc-Karp, G., & Zakrajsek, D.B. (1987). Planning for learning: Theory into practice. *Journal of Teaching in Physical Education,* **6**(4), 377-392.

Housner, L.D., & Griffey, D.C. (1985). Teacher cognition: Differences in planning and interactive decision making between experienced and inexperienced teachers. *Research Quarterly for Exercise and Sport,* **56**(1), 45-53.

Imwold, C.H., & Hoffman, S.J. (1983). Visual recognition of a gymnastic skill by experienced and inexperienced instructors. *Research Quarterly for Exercise and Sport,* **54**(2), 149-155.

Suggested Readings

American Alliance for Health, Physical Education, Recreation and Dance. (1983). *Physical education and sport for the secondary school student*. Reston, VA: Author.

American Alliance for Health, Physical Education, Recreation and Dance. (1984). *Tennis: Group instruction*. Reston, VA: Author.

Baschnagel, N. (1987). Thirty-minute indoor fundamental workout. *The Tennis Clinic*, January/February, **2**(3), 2.

Brewer, L. (1985). *Professional tennis drills*. New York, NY: Charles Scribner's Sons.

Brown, J. (1978). *Tennis without lessons*. Englewood Cliffs, NJ: Prentice-Hall.

Brown, J. (1980). *Tennis: Strokes, strategy, and programs*. Englewood Cliffs, NJ: Prentice-Hall.

Burke, M. (1986). Practicing in a gym. *The Tennis Clinic*, November/December, **2**(2), 6.

Lumpkin, A. (1985). *A guide to the literature of tennis*. Westport, CT: Greenwood Press.

Petro, S. (1986). *The tennis drill book*. Champaign, IL: Leisure Press.

United States Tennis Association. (1984). *USTA schools program tennis curriculum*. Princeton, NJ: Author.

United States Tennis Association. (1986). *The official United States Tennis Association 1986 yearbook*. Lynn, MA: H.O. Zimman.

Yamaha International Sporting Goods Division. (1987). *How to select the right tennis racquet*. Buena Park, CA: Author.

About the Author

Jim Brown is a professor of health and physical education at McNeese University in Lake Charles, Louisiana. He began playing tennis more than 35 years ago and has experience as a teaching professional, a college instructor and coach, a city program director, a writer and publisher, a consultant, and a clinician. He has written, coauthored, or edited 8 books and more than 50 articles on a variety of health and physical education topics. Dr. Brown has represented the United States Tennis Association, the American Alliance for Health, Physical Education, Recreation and Dance, and the President's Council on Physical Fitness and Sports in clinics throughout the United States and Mexico. In addition to his teaching duties at McNeese, he is the director of the McNeese Community Tennis Program and a member of the Wilson Sporting Goods tennis advisory staff.